# Be With Your Horse

## Getting to the heart of horsemanship

### TOM WIDDICOMBE

# Be With Your Horse

# Your Horse

## TOM WIDDICOMBE

David and Charles

## Acknowledgements

Many thanks to Jane for asking me to write this book, Jo
for editing it, and Sarah for making sure I got it right.

A DAVID & CHARLES BOOK
David & Charles is a subsidiary of F+W (UK) Ltd.,
an F+W Publications Inc. company

First published in the UK in 2005

Distributed in North America
by F+W Publications, Inc.
4700 East Galbraith Road
Cincinnati, OH 45236
1-800-289-0963

A catalogue record for this book is available from the British Library.

ISBN 0 7153 2020 3

Horse care and riding is not without risk, and while the author and publishers have
made every attempt to offer accurate and reliable information to the best of their
knowledge and belief, it is presented without any guarantee. The author and
publishers therefore disclaim any liability incurred in connection with using the
information contained in this book.

For more information about Tom Widdicombe's work with horses visit his website at
www.bewithyourhorse.com

Contact illustrator Lucy Turmaine through www.lucyturmaineportraits.co.uk

Printed in Malta by Gutenberg Press Ltd
for David & Charles
Brunel House      Newton Abbot      Devon

Commissioning Editor Jane Trollope
Desk Editor Louise Crathorne
Project Editor Jo Weeks
Production Controller Jennifer Campbell

Visit our website at www.davidandcharles.co.uk

David & Charles books are available from all good bookshops; alternatively you can
contact our Orderline on (0)1626 334555 or write to us at FREEPOST EX2 110,
David & Charles Direct, Newton Abbot, TQ12 4ZZ (no stamp required UK mainland).

# Be With Your Horse

## Getting to the heart of horsemanship

# • A way of being

*Think back to a time when you knew nothing about horses, a time when there wasn't a single thought in your head about how to be with them – for some people that time might even be now.*

And think of all the knowledge about horses that you now have – some of you might have none. This is the knowledge that you have accumulated over the years, months, weeks or days of being with horses in your life so far. Some of your knowledge has come from people, some has come from books, some has come from the horses themselves. Some of your knowledge works, some doesn't. Some of your knowledge is true, some isn't. Some of your knowledge is useful, some is useless – and some is worse than useless. Some knowledge is downright dangerous. Some things seem to work with some horses but not with others. Some things seem to work one day with one horse but then not work the next day with the same horse. And then there are some people for whom things seem to work well most of the time, and with most of the horses, and other people for whom nothing seems to work out very well ever, with any horse, and then there are all the people in between.

Within the huge spectrum of horse-related experiences, from donkeys on the beach to competition horses flying over huge jumps, each of us is working out part of our own destiny with horses. For some people it is just something going on in their lives that doesn't require much thought – for others it becomes a subject of almost infinite interest. And on top of all this, each individual horse that is brought by us into the world of human contact is trying to make some sense of what is going on, too.

# Soft ropes, soft hands, soft horses

When I'm working with a horse I like to use a nice soft rope, and I like to have a nice soft feel in my hands. Every job I do, I like to go into it with the softest approach I can to get the result I want. I try to get my message over to the horse in the most polite and gentle way possible.

The feel in your hands is a very powerful tool. It is a really big part of the communication that goes on between the handler and the horse. The messages you send to your horse through the rope can easily make the difference between getting a good result and getting no result at all. At first you may have to train your hands to feel the response of your horse, and then one day you will realize that you are feeling it without thinking about it.

What you are feeling is pressure and release, which is part of the language of the horse. It is not just an on/off switch but a whole spectrum of degrees of pressure, and the softer you are, the better it works. There is no fine tuning between a big tug and a huge tug – not that the horse can make much sense of, anyway – but get down to a gentle touch and then the horse can begin to listen to you. Suddenly softness can begin to flow both ways and communication begins to happen.

For some of us, this is what working or being with horses is all about – being in that moment and at one with your horse; feeling that understanding coming back to you, and the horse trying to figure out and do what you are asking him to do. And then you hear yourself say the words 'This is a nice horse', as if some horses aren't nice, or 'This horse really tries to get it right', as if some horses don't try to get it right. And then you begin to realize that maybe it's you who should be nice, and try to get it right, and maybe the horse isn't trying to get it right because he doesn't understand what you are asking him to get right. Perhaps only when you experience a horse communicate with you on the most simple level can you really begin to know that horses *are* 'nice' or that they really do try to get it right. This is their nature and maybe this is why we have become so involved with them.

So what is it that can bring the relationship between human and horse to the point of true co-operation? Is it the domain of only truly talented horsemen and women, or can it be learnt by anyone?

# The stallion man

One of the first horses my wife, Sarah, and I owned together was a young piebald colt. We kept him entire, as we had a couple of nice mares at the time that we wanted to get in foal. I had quite a time with that young horse; he was a real handful. In the end I asked a man I knew, who had a big stallion himself, if he could help me with him. He agreed, so I took my horse up to his yard. What happened next was the exact point in time when I first started to wonder if maybe I could find a successful way of being with horses. The man took the horse, and the horse just stood there quietly with him. I saw him do nothing, and when I asked him what he was doing he said he didn't know.

Over the next few weeks it really played on my mind that the stallion man didn't know what he was doing. Whatever it was, it was something very powerful that I certainly wasn't doing. I watched him very carefully, which should have given me some clues. He was a solid little chap, very quiet with the horse; he hardly took any notice of him, really. One day we took the colt to a show, and as we were waiting for our class the man asked me to hold the horse while he fetched his jacket. I was so nervous, but I had no idea what to do about it. I patted the horse on the neck and talked to him, trying to tell him everything was fine. Thankfully the stallion man was back in no time and I handed him the rope with a huge feeling of relief.

I knew that soon the horse would be back with me, so I asked the stallion man again 'What should I do if this horse gets wound up?' 'Oh, you'll be all right, he's quiet as a lamb now,' he replied. If only he could just have given me some practical advice – anything at all would have been good. I had no idea what I needed to do, and he had no idea what he was doing anyway so he couldn't tell me.

Our horse stayed at that yard for six weeks and when we got him back things were a little better between us. But as the days went by things began to drift, and before long it was as if the horse had never been away. I was back where I started and the truth of the matter began to hit me. It was *me* that was the problem – I simply did not have what it takes to be a successful horseman.

• • •

When I think back to the utter chaos I went through with that horse, and the total lack of knowledge I had about how to deal with it, the whole situation fills me with horror. The 'tools' at my disposal were few – basically a stick and my voice, neither of which did much more than add to the confusion the horse was already experiencing.

The following years were not easy. I loved my horses, but I could not forget about my failure as a horseman. I wanted to be good but I didn't know how. I tried this and that, but deep down I knew that there was something I lacked and the horses knew it too. My favourite horses were the ones that didn't take too much advantage of my weakness, and I didn't like the ones that did. It was all a very grey area. Were some horses good and others bad? Were the good ones good because someone else had already done the work that I couldn't do? Was it all in the breeding? Did I just need more experience? Should I go and work in a professional yard? On and on, the questions kept coming.

● If you can find a way to be with your horse when once you didn't have that way, then you will be a very good horseman or woman. You will be stronger for not having known, for realizing it, and for doing something about it. Several years later, I advertised a horse for sale and by chance it was the stallion man who turned up to buy him. He was still good – but hey, I knew so much more. I understood what was going on, I could explain it and teach it if anyone wanted to know it. I was doing it because I knew what I was doing and I was conscious of the horse. It felt good.

## It looks like magic!

We are waiting in the yard, just a bit anxious about our next visitor – one of those jobs to which I should perhaps have said no. Then here the horse is, coming up the drive, a lead rope fastened to either side of his halter and two people hanging on, attempting to keep some kind of order to the proceedings. The hot and bothered owner seems mighty relieved to have made it into the yard, and everything about her is screaming at me to take her horse. 'Here's Jake,' she says, 'where do you want him?'

'Give him to me for a second while we have a chat about what's going on here between you two,' I reply.

I take the horse and, forgetting the stories I have heard about him, I relax the rope and stand talking to the owner and her friend. The horse stands there perfectly still and I feel slightly awkward as they start to repeat the horror stories I heard on the phone the night before. As we talk I move the horse about a bit, nice and gently, back a step or two, a step to the side, and forward and halt, but mostly I just stand still. After a few minutes, I quietly take him into the stable, take off his halter and leave him to get used to his new surroundings.

*'Then here the horse is, coming up the drive, a lead rope fastened to either side of his halter and two people hanging on, attempting to keep some kind of order to the proceedings.'*

'Jake seems to like you, doesn't he? He never stands still like that for anyone,' says the owner. At that point I half expect her to ask me if I want to keep him, but thankfully it doesn't come to that.

'Well, let's see how he goes over the next few days, shall we?' I say, thinking that maybe I should spare them my theories of horse psychology and the effect of restrictive ropes on the horse's mind.

Now, of course I knew that in the days to come we would see the other side of that horse, and to a degree we did. But from the second I met him, and I was in charge of him, he knew that I knew a bit about what he needed in his life in order to feel comfortable – and one of those things was that he needed to feel free.

Horses are very sensitive creatures. Out of necessity, they are very finely tuned to respond to any threat from their environment – a second's delay in fleeing from danger could mean the difference between life and death. The number one instinct for a prey animal is survival: they are food and they know it. Horses will always try to set themselves up for the maximum chance of safety. Their best defence is the quickness of their reactions and the speed at which they can run away from danger.

These survival instincts are lodged deep in the mind of the horse. Let's get real: most horses don't really have to worry about being eaten by lions and tigers, but deep down in their DNA they don't know that, do they? That's why in the herd there will usually be one horse keeping lookout, or when you're out riding and a dog suddenly runs out from behind a hedge, most horses will react to some degree or another.

There are some things that will never ever change about horses and these are their basic instincts. They are the same in every horse. If we take on board without question that self-preservation is the main unchangeable and ever-present feature in the horse's mind, then we can begin to understand how and why the horse reacts to the environments into which we put him.

So why was Jake so concerned about his survival, to the extent that his behaviour was almost unmanageable, and why did his behaviour change so dramatically in seconds when he arrived at our yard? When he was with his owners, he was very aware that they were unable to provide him with the security that for him is an absolute necessity. In a similar way, but for slightly different reasons, Jake's owners were extremely worried about their own survival, too. They knew that they didn't have what Jake needed and in the circumstances they rightly felt very vulnerable indeed, and it showed.

If you can find out what it is that a horse needs and show him that you know about that, the behaviour of your horse will almost certainly change for the better. In this situation your confidence will begin to grow, and you and your horse can start getting some good work done.

## Making an impression

A good few years ago I took a mare to a nearby local stud. The owner of the stud was an old guy called George who over the years had been extremely successful with his horses at the top level of showjumping and eventing. He was a well-respected horseman. While I was waiting around with my mare, it became clear to me that George was a very busy man with a lot of important clients. Anyway, three weeks later I took the mare back to be scanned to see if she was in foal. All was well, I paid my money and returned home.

A couple of years later I was at a local yard that was selling up. There were plenty of people there and the horses were going for a lot of money. I was just standing around with Sarah when George came up and started discussing the horses with me. We had a pleasant conversation, albeit slightly one-sided because George obviously knew far more about horses than I did. I was expecting him just to say a couple of things and move on, but he didn't. We stood and talked for a long time. I listened with interest to what George had to say and he listened carefully to me. For a good half hour we both enjoyed each other's company. Eventually the sale came to an end and we said our goodbyes.

As George walked off, I glanced at Sarah with a questioning look on my face. She just said, 'He must think you're someone else!'

• • •

When you first meet a horse that you've never met before, in one way you are starting off with a blank canvas in terms of the relationship, in that nothing has happened between you so far. On the other hand, both you and the horse do carry with you all the information and experience you have accumulated in your lives so far. In some cases, this will be a huge amount, built up over years.

You will have worked out the best ways to get what you want from a horse, and you will also be aware of the things that don't work so well for you. If you like affection from your horse, you will probably know where he likes you to stroke or rub him. You probably know that grooming him around the base of the withers with your fingers often stimulates a similar grooming response from him. If you want your horse to behave in a workman-like fashion, you will probably know that if you behave like that yourself, he is more likely to take on that attitude. In terms of negative behaviour, you will almost certainly know that sudden movements around your horse's head are counterproductive if you want to help him relax with you, and shouting and banging about are not good tactics either.

Your horse is not starting off with a blank canvas either, but for him it is quite a bit more difficult. Over his life he has met lots of different people, many of them reacting in very different ways to similar situations. It is much harder for him to work out what it is that controls the way a human behaves. Let's face it, we tend to struggle with that too. Somehow the horse has had to devise a way of being that accommodates the many and varied responses that are coming at him from all these people. For example, it may be that last time he stepped towards a person they stepped out of his way, so understandably he thinks this is what happens. So, with the next person he meets he tries the same thing, but this time it is someone who finds this unacceptable. They shout and push and hit, so the horse quickly has to work out what is happening and look for a way of sorting out why all hell has broken loose and how he can bring some order back into the situation. He decides to try taking a step back away from the person and the mayhem subsides. When he meets person number three he has a real dilemma on his hands, because he is unsure whether or not he should move forward or back. In this example he will probably choose to move back, as he will not want to risk seeing all that confusion again. And guess what – the previous handler is probably congratulating themselves for sorting out a bargy horse, and good luck to them, in this instance their training method has worked.

• • •

A while ago we were asked to do some work with a couple of unhandled six-month-old Exmoor foals, so we travelled up to Exmoor to pick them up. Our job was to get them halter-trained. It sounds easy enough, and it was quite easy, but that is not the point of the story. These foals are born out on Exmoor and in the autumn the herd is gathered up for weaning. The first contact they have with humans is when they are caught and held still by several large men, checked for white hairs and to see if their feet have any white markings, and then, if they meet the standards set down by the breed society, they are held tightly and branded on two separate areas of their bodies with hot irons. A day or two later they are taken from their mothers, who are then turned back out onto the moor.

So, what information do these foals have about humans? When the ponies arrived with us, the brand marks were a suppurating mess and the ponies were wild as hell. The wildness was fair enough – they probably would have been that way anyway – but when it came to getting them to accept us we couldn't help feeling that maybe it was all a little bit harder than it needed to be. In the noble cause of balanced writing, I have to say those ponies came really good for us, and over the years I have seen some superb Exmoors giving people a lot of pleasure. It could be argued that those ponies' first impressions of humans were neither here nor there, and 'all's well that ends well'. I give all credit to the qualities of the horse – it is amazing that we can do such things to them and still they come back and serve us in the way they do.

• • •

When you first meet your horse he may have a few ideas about you, but in most cases I have found it is a good idea to get in there early and show the horse a couple of small things, and he will soon take on board that you are a fair-minded person with whom he can work just fine. Remember, the horse wants to survive and he wants a peaceful life – he's not over-bothered about much else. When you first meet your horse, he doesn't know whether you're the next great trainer on the block or just another person passing through. Not only does he not know, he doesn't care either – nor does it matter. You don't need special powers, or a super-high IQ, or a degree in science, or to have worked in the Midwest with the old cowboys who have 'forgotten more about horses than you'll ever know', or to have read the old books by the masters. All you need to know, anyone can know.

Of course, for some people things will be easier than for others. There is no doubt that some people are almost born horse people. I once heard a trainer described as half-man half-horse, which I thought was going a bit over the top. But I do concede there are some people who are naturally good with horses – the rest of us are just average beings trying to find a way through. I know for sure I am in this category. I get huge pleasure from watching top horse people at work, but I also get huge pleasure from working horses the way I do, and from watching people who have maybe struggled with horses but who are starting to put together some good stuff, just because they are beginning to understand how to offer the horse what he really wants – some good clear and consistent communication.

● Communication is a remarkably powerful thing: if the horse knows that you know, then you're on your way. Look at it from the other point of view: if the horse knows that you don't know, then he has every right to worry. He is basically 'on his own', and that is one place the horse does not want to be. If you can show the horse that you are with him, taking care of him and you are not going to let him down, then he will start to put his trust in you.

By the way, the last sentence does not mean 'yes I'm standing next to him, yes I'm feeding him and keeping him warm, and yes I've been doing this for years'. 'With him' means that you are there right now, very aware that he is there and very aware that he does not want to be on his own. 'Taking care of him' means being the leader, freeing him from the responsibility of looking after himself so that he can relax. 'Not letting him down' means providing this care consistently so that he can really begin to rely on you. This is

**what he is after. So, from the moment you begin to work with your horse, you can begin to establish in his mind that you can provide him with these requirements, and from then on in this relationship that is how you proceed.**

# The travelling horseman

A few years ago, I was driving into town when I saw a bowtop caravan on the roadside verge with two horses tethered nearby. There was a cardboard sign stuck up on a stick saying 'Work Wanted'. I saw the guy sitting there by his fire, so I pulled up for a chat. He introduced himself to me as Manny. He was travelling down to the Westcountry to visit his daughter. His wagon was pulled by a 15hh bay cob, and travelling alongside he had a nice two-year-old skewbald filly that he was training up for the future. We got on OK: I needed some hedging work done and Manny needed somewhere to put his horses, so I gave him a map of where I lived.

A few days later Manny and his wagon pulled into the yard. The first thing I noticed was the front feet of the young filly. Nowadays, it is becoming quite common to see horses wearing rubber boots on their front feet instead of metal shoes, but this was the first time I had ever seen it. Manny had simply cut the toes off some wellies, modified them and tied them on with strips of cloth. His system was working a treat.

At the time, we had just begun our first year of working professionally with other people's horses. We were finding the whole thing quite stressful. A short while before, horses had been just a hobby, but this was working for other people, for real money, with their real horses, and the responsibility was weighing quite heavily. We worked pretty hard that first year and we didn't have any money to show for it. Business is not really my scene – it's taken me a long time to sort of understand how it works. You buy something for less and sell it for more, the difference is the profit, and that's what you live on. But don't forget to add on your expenses, they have to come out of that bit too. Forty years into my working life and I'm still missing this one now and again.

Anyway, let's get back to Manny. We had to walk the horses about a mile to get to the field and on the way we had to cross a stream. The old horse walked through without a problem, but the youngster decided she couldn't manage it and for some reason I felt it was my responsibility to get her to the other side. One thing I didn't really like when we first started our business was that hanging over me all the time was this dreadful expectation that I had to know all the answers and all the ways out of all the problems. I know the feeling was coming from within me, but it somehow seemed to go with the territory. It took me quite a few years to escape from that feeling and even now it still pops up from time to time. Nowadays, I don't go into jobs expecting to know all the answers: if the answers are going to come, they seem to come out of the way that we work.

So there we were, stuck at this stream. I took the lead rope and worked with the filly for a while, and after a few minutes she decided to give it a go. We walked back and forth through the stream half a dozen more times to make sure she was OK with it, and then we carried on to the field. On the walk home I was hit by a barrage of questions from Manny: what was I doing, how did I do it, where did I learn it? On and on it went.

Over the next few weeks I realized that I had met someone who I can only describe as being desperate to learn about horses. Manny was like a sponge sucking up information. One thing I remember about him in those early days, and I know he won't mind me saying this, is that he was so desperate to learn it all that he just tried too hard. He wanted to communicate with the horses in their 'language', he wanted results, he really wanted to get it right. Maybe in their place these are all noble and correct aims, but

*'So there we were, stuck at this stream. I took the lead rope and worked with the filly for a while, and after a few minutes she decided to give it a go.'*

in the first couple of weeks he tried so hard and everything was so exaggerated that the horses just looked at him and wondered what on earth he was doing. I recall more than once reassuring him that everything would come good and to keep in mind that some things take time.

Manny is a really good horseman. As the years go by our paths still cross occasionally. A few months ago we had a conversation where he was telling me how he feels about horses now. I came away amazed that we went off on our separate journeys, but still ended up in the same place – when it comes to working with horses, it's how we are, not what we do.

# Do you really need to know?

Many people have tried to explain their successful relationships with horses by working out the dynamics of the herd and fitting themselves into the appropriate position in the hierarchy. These methods assume that humans can take on the role of a horse to such an extent that horses assimilate them into their experience as being just like another horse. This may not be as far fetched as it sounds. We certainly do it the other way around, when we imagine that horses think in a human way and expect them to respond to situations in the way we do. But why do we have to justify everything with theories? If, say, a horse backs out of our space, why do we then have to turn around and say 'Ah, that's what happens in the herd between the alpha and beta horses' or whatever? The theory may be correct, and there's no harm in knowing it, but is it actually of any consequence? If something works for me, do I really need to know the reason why? If I'm not going to eat to end my hunger or stand up to stretch my legs until I understand the process of how it works... well, I wouldn't get out of bed in the morning using that kind of logic.

People joust intellectually with each other to justify and prove their training methods, but you don't have to go far to find a good horseman who knows nothing of the theory. In the days when thousands of men and horses worked as the main source of power, there were good horsemen among them who knew how to get the best from their horses. These guys weren't educated or clever, they could just feel for their horse, and the horse would respond. If we can find the common ground where we can communicate in a real and meaningful way with the horse, then we can achieve the same results.

So, I don't think we have to pretend to be a horse and I'm not sure that we can speak to them in their 'language' either. A friend of mine seriously got into the idea of designing remote control clip-on horse ears that would enable him to communicate more easily with his horse. OK, he'd had an ale or two, but just imagine things the other way around, where the horse has to learn our language – even if he could think in words, he couldn't physically say them. I have watched and read about animal communicators who pass on messages from horses and can even do it over the phone. These powers are way beyond my understanding, but I can definitely work out some of the things my horse is feeling. I can see when he is cross: that's easy, his ears go right back and I feel a bit threatened. I can see when he likes being groomed: he leans into it and kind of squirms around enjoying the sensation. But once you start to realize the primary importance of the horse's instinct for survival, you don't need to know too much about the specifics of what this means and what that means. For example, if your horse won't go in the trailer, would it actually help if he could tell you that he's not too happy about going into small spaces, that in fact he is claustrophobic, and what's more the last time he went in he didn't like the feel of the rubber sides as he was travelling at speed around corners? Not really. All you need to know is that the horse doesn't feel comfortable about going into the trailer, he feels in danger, and your job is simply to show him that things are going to be OK.

⬤ So often the problems actually start from our incorrect interpretation of what the horse is going through at any one moment. People often say things like 'Well, he knows what I want him to do, he's done it hundreds of times and there's absolutely no reason for him not to do it. He's just being pig-headed!' This is a very human interpretation of horse logic, based almost entirely on the human perspective on the world. Once you begin to try to look at life from the horse's point of view, however, these thoughts are much less likely to happen. Because we are humans, inevitably our tendency is to put human interpretations on everything that happens, but from the perspective of the horse this is often not very helpful.

Let's use loading into a trailer as an example. In this situation there are usually two very different interpretations of what is going on – the view of the people involved, and the view of the horse. If you watch someone having a problem loading their horse, you can pick up a lot of useful information about both human and horse psychology. One thing that commonly happens is that the person behind the horse puts some pressure on him – for example, they might hit him with a stick. The horse moves forward to get away from the stick and the person thinks, 'Oh, that seems to be working,' so they hit him again. This tells the horse that moving forward doesn't get away from the stick at all, so he stops and tries to find some other way out. The stick keeps coming, so the horse runs out to the side or pulls backwards as far as possible, and yes, that seems to have got rid of the stick for a moment. The handlers line up the horse again and then use the stick again, so now that tells the horse that even lining up for the trailer is not a good idea, and on and on it goes. Before they know it, they've got a real loading problem on their hands. If only a bit more time and care had been taken at the point where the horse first showed them that he was a little worried about going into the trailer, things could have turned out very differently.

Now let's look back at the human response to the horse moving forward after he was hit for the first time. The person's reaction was correct in a way, because they did something and things started to move in the right direction, so they automatically thought that the best idea was to keep doing it. Why change a winning formula? Unfortunately, this automatic human interpretation is exactly 180 degrees opposite to the interpretation of the horse, and so the problems begin. If we can train ourselves to see things from the horse's point of view, then we can actually override this incorrect response and start to get some good results with our horses.

Over the years we have loaded lots of young horses that we have bred on our farm. Never have I found even one of them to be a naturally bad loader. Bad loaders are not born, generally they are made by people misunderstanding the nature of the horse and failing him in his moment of need. Of course, accidents happen and sometimes circumstances beyond our control can create problems. Maybe as your horse goes into the trailer for the first time, there is a huge gust of wind and a branch falls from a tree and smashes onto the trailer roof. Fair enough, any horse is quite rightly going to question the wisdom of going into the trailer again after that. So what should we do if that did happen? What I would do is start again and try to show the horse that in fact it is OK to go into the trailer, and that his first experience is not something that happens every time. A good tip here would be to avoid working on this problem on a windy day, or under a dodgy tree. I know it sounds obvious, but these sorts of basic mistakes can be made all too easily.

# One job to do

Is it really possible to work successfully with horses and yet be blissfully unaware of the many training theories and techniques that surround the whole subject? Could there be one thing by which, if we knew it, everything else would fall into place – a sort of 'Holy Grail' for horses?

When I was growing up I wasn't the brightest kid in the class, and I knew that my destiny included finding a way through life that wasn't going to require a super intellect. I didn't have one available, so my options on that front were obviously limited. Not only that, but I took a good look at the cleverer kids in the class and, in some cases, I was not over-impressed. Mercifully, it seemed to me that the most important things in life were not linked to measurable qualities like intellect, good looks or wealth. There were two things that motivated me: firstly, I wanted to be comfortable with the people around me, and secondly, I didn't want anyone on my case.

When I read that last sentence, I can't help thinking how similar my needs were then to those of the horses that I work with today. Pretty much every horse needs to feel that he is part of a herd; he also needs to know where he fits into that herd. And he really doesn't want any other horse, or person for that matter, on his case. In the established herd there may be the odd skirmish now and again, but they are soon over. The overriding desire of the herd members is for a peaceful existence.

Horse trainers come through town selling their systems, and we all go and watch. Of course, it's well worthwhile because we learn a bit of this and a bit of that. But if we distil it down, take out the add-ons, and have a really close look at why some people are acclaimed as being 'good with horses', then we can start to see the magic ingredient, the essence of good horsemanship. What we see in these people is the quality that enabled my stallion to relax in the presence of the stallion man. This is what we need to find in ourselves, and when we find it then we have what the horse needs. Without it, our interactions with horses will almost certainly be described using words like misunderstanding, difficulty and mystery.

• • •

I once worked with a girl for several weeks. Debby was very keen to learn and to improve her horsemanship. To be honest, she knew way more about some aspects of horses than I did. She was a very experienced competitive rider and since childhood she had known that working with horses was all she wanted to do. She was very sincere about what she was doing with her life, and everything she did was carried out to a very high professional standard. I enjoyed having her around and we did some good work together. But when she left I was disappointed – not because she had gone, but because in all the time she was with me I had not been able to get across to her the way that I felt horses like us to be.

One day we were working with a young pony who was a little tired of people trying to sort out his life. He had come to us (as they did at that time) to be put 'back on the rails'. I was working in the round pen with the pony and things were going well. When I work with horses, I tend to concentrate on very simple stuff; this is the best way to get my message across to the horse. (When I told Sarah I had been asked to write a book, without hesitation she replied, 'The way you work with horses could be written on the back of a postage stamp.' On one level I felt very aggrieved, but in reality it was a back-handed compliment. What she meant to imply is that I work in a very simple way. At least, that is what she said when I let her know I was somewhat taken aback by her remark.) I was just practising a bit of leading, and a bit of stop and start. It was good and the pony was with me, so in my wisdom I decided to turn him loose. Now, I knew this pony had a catching problem and in hindsight I should have known better than to let him go. I can't remember why, but there was quite a crowd around that day, and as I went to catch the pony I quickly realized that I had made a bit of an error. I didn't stand a chance, and for some reason I got a bit flustered and began to feel the pressure of the situation. Two or three people called out that they would have a go, and before I knew it, Debby was in there trying to catch the pony.

Now, I know that there are all sorts of techniques for catching uncatchable horses and I'm sure they're all fine. I use a technique myself – I quietly walk towards the pony, and then when he walks off, what I do is... No, I'm not going to tell you what I do, not right now anyway, because this book is not primarily about techniques. It is not designed as a manual where you can go to the index, look up catching problems, and read about 'my methods'. This book is about how to be, in such a way that you can naturally find an effective way to deal with each individual situation.

Back to Debby's technique. It didn't work, and then she started getting all sorts of advice from the other people watching – they all had their techniques, too. After a few minutes Sarah stepped in and decided that before the pony got too wound up about being caught, she should have a go. I have to say it was a catching masterclass, and I defy anyone to see the 'system' she was using. She just read that horse, she could feel that pony and the pony could feel her, and in a couple of minutes the job was done and the pony was happy.

'How did you do that? What were you doing?' The inquest went on for quite a while. I don't know if any conclusions were reached, but I do know that beyond all the 'ways of doing it' was what really happened. That is what I wanted to get across to Debby, and in those few weeks during which we worked together I didn't manage it.

I think one of the reasons why I couldn't get this idea over was that for Debby it was all about 'how to do it', and on several occasions that was not what was needed at all. For instance, one time we were doing some ridden work with a young horse and I couldn't work out why he was struggling with such a simple thing as backing up. Over and over I tried to get Debby simply to ask the horse back with a light feel on the reins, but the horse just didn't seem to be getting it. Eventually I asked Debby exactly what she was doing, and – I don't know why I was so surprised – she had so much going on there that the horse didn't stand a chance. Weight changes, leg movements, visualization, and what I was asking her to do with her hands – all the stuff she had learnt in her life so far, plus some new stuff that she was throwing in as well to see if that would help, and all the poor little horse needed was a bit of simple 'feel'. And, sadly, all Debby needed was a bit of simple 'feel' too, but she was so obsessed with all the techniques that the feel just couldn't get through.

## You can do it

When the telephone rings and the person on the end of the line starts to tell me about some difficulties they are having with their horse, I quite often listen to the caller and wonder how on earth I could help anyone out with a situation like that. I usually end up saying that I am more than happy to come and take a look, but right now I'm not sure how I would deal with the problem. This feeling often sticks with me right up to the moment when I actually start to work with the horse. And then, most times at least, the feeling drops away and I find something we need to do and we get on with the job.

That is a beautiful feeling: when you know there is something you can work on with your horse, and that things are going to get better. You start to see that his life is going to become easier, and as he begins to realize that you are someone he can work with, he starts to see that too. Take the time that is needed to get the job done.

Abandon thoughts of the smaller goal – sorting out the symptoms – and set your sights on the feeling of being with your horse right now. It's a timeless experience and it feels good.

● There are a few simple principles that allow this experience to happen, and for sure these principles can be applied using systems or techniques. But there is a danger that goes with this, in that we can start to believe it is the system that produces the results, rather than the communication that is going on within the system. How many times have you seen people bashing on and on with a system because the horse isn't responding in the way that they want him to? If the system states that the horse must move away from twirling ropes, then do you just make that happen at all costs? How much sweeter to gently ask your horse to move over and have him do it because he wants to be with you and to work with you. That spirit of co-operation is within every horse, but we must play our part. We must offer our half of the deal. We must learn to distinguish between an ask and a tell, try to feel it in our hands and in the way we are around our horse. When we get it right he will let us know – he will be happy to move over or lift his feet or do whatever job we ask of him.

A couple of years back, I spent an all too short a time watching a top trainer and one of his favourite sayings at the time was 'you get what you settle for'. It's absolutely true when it comes to horses. Let's settle for the best. Let's get our horses so that they are happy to be around us and happy to go places with us. What that means is let's simply set up this relationship between us and the horse so that it works this way. It's not an impossible dream or the privilege of the few – it is well within the reach of everyone. Do you really want to settle for less?

# The Holy Grail

Once upon a time, many, many centuries ago, there was a very remote kingdom far away from any other civilization. It was a long and perilous journey to reach this kingdom, so it was not often that anyone from the outside world arrived at their gates. However, one day an adventurous young merchant arrived with his mule, and across the mule's back was a small roll of luxurious carpet.

It so happened that at this time the kingdom was ruled by a ruthless and very selfish king, and when he heard about the merchant's arrival he demanded that he be brought to the palace immediately. When the king saw the carpet he was intrigued – never before had he experienced anything but bare floors. He walked around on the carpet and jumped up and down with joy. And then without further ado he proclaimed to his courtiers: 'This carpet is wonderful and I have decided that from this day on my whole kingdom shall be carpeted, so that wherever I walk my feet will be safe from danger.'

A few brave courtiers tried to explain to the king that his request was not reasonable, but he was determined that he should get his way. He began to get very angry and started threatening all sorts of unpleasantness if steps weren't taken immediately towards fulfilling his desires.

It so happened that travelling with the merchant was a very wise man, and seeing the situation deteriorating and the imminent danger that he and his friend were in, he decided to intervene. 'Dear king,' he said, 'I perfectly understand that wherever you walk you want carpet beneath your feet, that is indeed not a problem.' Now this was the kind of talk that the king liked to hear. 'Little old man,' he said, 'if you can provide me with my wish then I will make you very rich.'

'To see you happy will be more than enough a reward for me,' said the wise man, much to the annoyance of his friend the merchant, who was beginning to wonder if he might be in line for a bit of a windfall. 'Fetch me some scissors and I'll see what I can do.' By now everyone was getting very excited, wondering how the little old man was going to satisfy the needs of the king. More than anything, there was a great sense of relief that the attention was well and truly on the old man, and should he fail in his promise then the likelihood was that he alone would pay the price for the king's disappointment.

The old man took the scissors and cut out two pieces of carpet just a bit bigger than the king's feet and strapped them onto the king. 'Now good king, wherever you walk in your kingdom you will be walking on carpet,' he said. 'You alone are truly fortunate.'

The king was delighted. He paid the merchant handsomely for the carpet and everyone was thankful to the old man for once again restoring happiness to the kingdom. And so it is with your horse, if you get one simple thing right – how you are – then everything else will be so much easier.

# • Setting up the relationship

*There are many ways of training horses, and there are a lot of trainers and owners out there doing some really good work. I do not believe that there is only one right way of training a horse, nor do I believe that any one way is necessarily better than any other. I do believe, however, that it is important that we find a way of working with our horses that suits us, that we are comfortable with, and that helps us reach whatever goals we want to achieve with our horses.*

For me, the number one job I have to do with my horse is to set up a good relationship with him. This job is not one that, once done, can then be forgotten about – it is an ongoing process that requires attention whenever I am with my horse. For their own safety, horses are continually checking out their situation, including everyone and everything around them. They're not unlike us in that respect, are they? But remember that the first preoccupation in the horse's mind is his own survival. The state of his relationship with you is a reflection of your worth in his eyes in terms of his own safety.

If, in the eyes of your horse, you are not up to the job of looking after him (and I'm going to say it again, here we are not talking about mucking out and providing him with sweet hay), then he will not be able to relax with you. He won't feel safe and, probably even worse for you, he may well feel the need to start taking care of himself. Fortunately, there are some really simple things that you can do to show your horse you are well up to the job of looking after him, and this is what this chapter is all about.

● Remember that whenever you are with your horse, you are training your horse. You may not be training him to do something good, but you will be training him to do something. If you bear this fact in mind, then it does begin to look as if it may be a good idea to have some kind of strategy for producing positive results.

Some people are surprised by the level of concentration I ask for when they are working with me and their horses. Many of you will have a vision of sitting on your horse ambling down country lanes or wandering across the moors, the sun on your back, birds singing, without a care in the world. The last thing you want is some trainer telling you to concentrate on what you are doing, or to be really aware of the signals that you may inadvertently be giving to your horse. As I write this, I'm thinking myself that maybe I've got it wrong and yes, I too would like to relax once in a while with my horse. But that's the point – that's what started me off on this whole thing because, yes, I would like to relax with my horse, but I have realized that for me to be able to relax with my horse, I have to make sure that my horse can relax with me.

Of course, you may be one of those people who seem naturally to encourage horses to relax in your presence, or maybe you're lucky and own one of those horses that is just easy to be with. But if you're not in that situation then, hopefully, the next few pages will give you a good insight into some of the ways in which you can make real improvements in the relationship you have with your horse.

There are two very simple rules – I hesitate to use the word 'rules', maybe 'guidelines' would be better – to use when setting up your relationship with your horse. First, be in control of the movement, and second, establish your personal space. Now I don't know if this is what horses do in the herd and, as I said earlier, in a way I don't care either. If it works, and you are comfortable doing it, does it really matter why it works? When I first realized that things can be that simple, I couldn't really believe it. Even now, after nearly every job we go to, I end up getting into the car and saying to Sarah, 'I can't believe it works like that.' I usually say it a couple more times on the way home as well, until she tells me I'm getting a bit like a stuck record: 'Can't you move it on a bit?' 'But I don't seem to be able to – I just can't believe it is as simple as that!'

## Was he just a bad loader?

I got called out to a really tricky job the other day. The horse was a bad loader. Whenever someone rings up about a loading problem I get a bit nervous – I always have this faint hope in my heart that they are going to say something along the lines of, 'It's amazing really that a Shetland pony can give us so much trouble!' Of course, in reality what I nearly always hear is that the horse in question is an extremely strong and very fit 17.2hh sports horse – mmm, lovely, just what I like!

This job was doubly interesting because Ruth, the owner, quite often could load Soldier – a large, fit sports horse – without a problem, but at other times found it impossible. The last time they went to an event, it took five hours to get the horse to go into the trailer for the return journey. Ruth's first words to me on the phone were, 'I need your help. My husband has told me that it's "make your mind up time": either the horse goes or he goes.' When I arrived at their yard, I was relieved to see that Ruth and Martin were in fact the sweetest people, so in reality I would not have been responsible for a broken marriage if I had been unable to do the job. But where do you start with a horse that sometimes does something and other times does not?

● I always approach a horse in a quiet manner. I usually give him a very gentle rub on the neck, put the halter on, and then ask him to take a step backwards. I do this by putting the lightest of pressure on the lead rope under the chin. This puts a little bit of pressure on the noseband, which the horse can feel. It's important to use only as much pressure as you need – remember to ask, not tell. The horse will try to find a way out of the pressure: he just can't not do this, it is absolutely in his nature. Most trained horses will very quickly work out that a step backwards is what you are after, and as they start to move in that direction I gently release the pressure. I do nothing else: one ask, one give from the horse, and one release from me. I don't add anything else – no words, no stroking, just quiet stillness or what I call 'nothing'.

So, what I have just achieved there is control of the movement. I have clearly shown the horse that I can ask him to move, and I have also clearly shown him that there is something in it for him when he does move. I usually do this two or three times in the first minute or so when I meet a new horse.

● I want to explain about 'nothing'. I like to establish really early on with a horse that there is a place where we can both be together where nothing is happening, where we both just stand quietly, together. This is the basis of everything I do. Horses feel safe there because there is no pressure and it is easy for them to understand that they are getting it right. It is also very easy for me to explain to them about this place, and this is how I do it.

When I stand with the horse, my intention is to establish in his mind that I have a personal space. Interestingly, sorting out personal space is also very high on the agenda of information that every horse needs to know for his own comfort too, and that is why this small procedure really works. I want my horse to know that there is an area around me that he is not allowed into unless he is invited. Exactly how much space I want between him and me depends a bit on the size of the horse. If he is a strapping 17hh hunter then I really don't want him too close to me: I'd like him to stand a good couple of feet away. So, as I stand there with my horse I wait for him to ask me about my space. As you probably know from experience, this 'ask' sometimes comes sooner rather than later and in a huge way, like a mighty barge right through you or a nicely aimed head butt. But generally, because of the work I have just been doing with the backing up, the horse is already beginning to cotton on to the fact that it might be me who calls the shots, and also that I might be someone worth checking out quietly, in response to the quiet approach I've made to him. A typical first ask from the horse might be a gentle approach with his nose towards my arm.

● One thing you really need to take on board is that if a horse asks you a question and you don't answer it, he will take that as a 'yes'. That is why if you want to train your horse well, whenever you are with him you must answer all his questions. If, when that horse asks you if it is all right to touch your arm, you do nothing, the horse will think, 'OK, I'm allowed there, so I'll just ask whether it's OK to go a bit further.' (I'd better point out that I'm pretty sure horses don't think in words like that – in fact, I'm certain they don't. Whenever I use words in this way it's because they describe quite well what I think is going on in the horse's head.) You don't answer that question either, so the horse moves on, and before you know it he's all over you. Even more important than his invasion of your personal space is the fact that you

**have just missed your golden opportunity to establish the relationship with your horse in the way that you want it, rather than vice versa.**

I know some people have problems with the political correctness of imposing their will over that of the horse and strive for an equal partnership. But this is a bit of a case of imagining that horses look at their lives in the same way as humans do. Most horses I've met are only too happy to hand over the responsibility of choice if they can find a good strong leader. They are horses, not humans, and we are humans, not horses. For most horse owners these finer ethical points are not a worry, so let's get back to working on personal space. The horse moves towards your arm and you need to tell him that he is crossing the line you have drawn around your space. I think that the best way to tell him is in a 'language' that he naturally understands, so what I do is just make a sudden movement – as little as it takes to get him to move back out of my space. As soon as he moves back, I return to 'nothing' and just stand there. The horse will look at me a bit surprised and within a few seconds will probably check me out again, just to make sure that my response wasn't some involuntary uncontrolled twitch left over from an old war injury. So, just as before, as he crosses the line, he receives exactly the same response, and now he is beginning to get the idea that I am some kind of consistent force which maybe he can rely on.

He may ask me the same question over and over, and I will keep answering it in the same way. Then there comes a time when he just thinks (and again, I don't think he thinks this in words) roughly along the lines of, 'Oh well, there's absolutely no point going over that line, because every time I do, there is a real sudden movement that I have to move back away from, and it's just too much hassle, I think I'll just stand still.' I then say, but not in words, 'Good idea mate, and to reward you I'll just stand still too.'

And that is how we set up the basis of our whole relationship. Now we have a really good arrangement where he knows, and I know, that if we both just stand still together, things get really easy. I am starting to establish a good base from which to work. I can build on this and, all in good time, I can work towards what the client might call the main job, but I what know is really the lesser job. In Ruth's case, the bad and erratic loading is in fact a symptom of a poorly done main job: setting up the correct relationship.

Of course, things are often trickier than this. Some horses are a lot more testing. They may have a history of barging through people, or just walking off whenever they feel like it. Some horses may need more of an answer to their questions than a swift shrug of the shoulders. When you answer your horse, it is important to make your answer proportionate to his question. Sometimes a more nervous horse will move back from just a look in the eye, whereas a horse that has never experienced anything other than pushing people around, and people pushing him around, may need a big reaction from you to produce a response – you have to read it as you go.

Whatever the response you are getting from your horse, one thing remains the same: your horse wants and needs to know, in black and white, how things stand between you and him. That is the key to a very big part of his well-being. I have noticed that even the most timid of horses appreciates knowing where the line is between you and him. Of course, if you go in 'all guns blazing' with a horse that is scared to death of you, you will only confirm that his initial feelings were correct, but if you adjust your answers so that he can cope with them, it really can help him to relax and accept that you are a good person to have around. I always start off small and gauge the reaction I get, then work from there.

• • •

Every horse has so much to teach you and so it was with Ruth and Martin's horse. I once again realized just how sensitive and responsive horses actually are: it is an ongoing lesson. I came away from that particular job marvelling at the different responses that Soldier gave to the pressure. There is a fine line between ask and tell, almost finer than a human can feel, but if we watch the horse and are sensitive to him, he will tell us exactly where that line is. If you cross the line, it often causes the horse to react in the opposite way to the one that you had hoped.

One thing I try to do is let the client work with the problem. It may be back tomorrow and I won't be there to help, so I got Martin to have a go before Soldier was loading without question. Soldier stopped at the ramp and I said, 'Just ask him forward.' As Martin put a bit of pressure on the rope, the horse leant backwards and got even more stuck. What Martin had done was *tell* rather than *ask*! We started again and I suggested he be really gentle and ask with the least amount of pressure he could use. The horse moved towards him like a dream.

When things are really flowing between you and your horse, then tasks become easy for both of you. If you want your horse to move over sideways, then there is just that correct touch that will get him to move over willingly without question. If you go beyond that touch, he may well push back, and then you may well push more... and the battle has begun.

# Keep your horse sweet

What this is all about is keeping your horse sweet. Gambler came to our yard last summer. He was a very pretty four-year-old quarter horse-cross that his owner Mary had bought to fulfil her dreams of western riding. Mary wanted nothing but the best for Gambler, and to that end she had sent him to be started at one of the most expensive yards in the area. Things didn't work out too well for Gambler, and several weeks later he was returned to Mary with the diagnosis that he had 'an attitude problem'.

I remember this job really clearly. There was a point early on where Mary almost gave me Gambler. I wanted him, too – he was a real good looker and as sensitive as you could ever want. It was one of those situations where the words coming out of my mouth should probably have been, 'I'll tell you what, Mary, to help you out of a jam, I'll take your horse on for you,' but I stood listening to myself in amazement as I actually said, 'I'll tell you what Mary, why don't we see how the job goes? Maybe when you see it working out you won't be so keen to be rid of him.'

Gambler was fine in the stable, with his pile of haylage and his bucket of water, but as soon as you went in there to put on his halter he got all fidgety and cross. However, the point at which his problems really showed up was at the moment when you tried to take him into the sand school. His ears went back and he became just a little bit intimidating all round. I know that when horses get like that it sometimes feels as if you should just get a bit cross back, and say, 'Look, we've just got to get on with this, so knuckle down and accept it.' I've done this occasionally and it's sorted things out to a degree, but I don't really recommend it. I knew a bit about Gambler's history, and I just had this feeling that his reluctance to go into the sand school was due to the fact that he associated the whole thing with something confusing and unpleasant that had happened there in the past.

● If a horse isn't happy with something, I'm not a great fan of just batting on. I like to get each step sorted out as I go. This is a much easier approach, because everything is in order and clear to see. Sometimes I think we tend to imagine that things are more difficult to sort out than they are, but if you

go right back to the beginning and then move forward one
step at a time, the job you have to do will often unfold before
your eyes. The other great advantage of working in this way
is that, more often than not, sorting out the small stuff also
sorts out the big stuff. That's got to be good whichever way
you look at it.

With Gambler, the first thing to show him was that me coming into
the stable and putting on his halter was not a problem. How easy
is that? No, really, think about it. How would you do it? If that is
the only job you have to do, and you have no agenda in your mind
beyond that, then how would you do it? This is the approach I try to
take to each job I do. So I went into the stable and Gambler started
off by being his usual grumpy self. I tried to do as little as possible,
and I quietly put on the halter, stood with him for a few seconds,
took it off, stood for a few more seconds and then walked out of
the stable. I needed to break the association in Gambler's mind that
having the halter put on was the prelude to something happening
that he didn't enjoy. He looked a bit surprised – I admit that look
may only have been in my imagination, but I don't think it was.
Who knows?

A few minutes later I went into the stable and put on the halter
again. It didn't take long for Gambler to realize that the whole thing
was no hassle at all to him.

Now, if you are thinking, 'My god, this is small stuff, when is he
going to get on with some real work?' well, I'll have to leave you
there, because as far as I'm concerned, yes, on one level it is small
stuff, but on the level where it counts, in the mind of the horse, it
is huge stuff. That simple first step is probably the biggest step of
the whole job. In the horse's mind we have started to break the
pattern which says that humans, and everything they want to do,
are a pain. We are going to try to show the horse that humans, and

everything they want to do, are not a problem at all, and in fact life with humans can be fun. Keep the horse sweet – why would you want it any other way?

Next, I had to show Gambler that coming out of the stable was not a problem to him; in fact it was quite the reverse. I gently asked him to follow me out of the stable, and in the yard I quietly groomed him for a few minutes, then put him back in the stable. Easy does it works a treat. In no time at all Gambler was more than happy to be around the place and everybody loved him. I know at this point many people – and I include myself here – would be saying, 'Ah yes, but just wait until you ask him to do something he doesn't want to do.' This is quite right, but here we have a very sour horse: are we really going to sweeten him up by giving him stuff to do that he doesn't like doing? People have tried that on him and it hasn't worked at all. There are two things going on here. First, we want our horse to enjoy what we ask him to do, and second, when we have to ask our horse to do stuff that he doesn't enjoy so much, we want him to be able to do it without a problem because he's doing it for us. You just won't get that kind of 'giving' out of a horse if you've buried it under a whole load of bad attitude, tedious work or, as is so often the case, fear.

A day or two later, with Gambler sweet as a nut, we tried to go into the sand school. Old memories die hard, and Gambler stuck on the way in. I gently asked him forwards and we got there on the second ask. I did one walk around in a small circle – remember, this was all still on the lead rope – then we returned to the stable and that was the end of another session. With every step we took Gambler was beginning to realize that things don't always stay the same: because something was bad once, that does not mean it is always going to be bad.

For the first few days of working with Gambler, with every new thing we did with him, we had to go through the same procedure.

*'When we put the saddle on he was really apprehensive about it. We put it on and took it off. We gently did up the girth and he was worried. We undid it and showed him, 'Look, it's not a problem,' and next time it wasn't.'*

When we put the saddle on he was really apprehensive about it. We put it on and took it off. We gently did up the girth and he was worried. We undid it and showed him, 'Look, it's not a problem,' and next time it wasn't. At this time I was working with Carrie, who is naturally a very quiet, caring rider, but still Gambler was expecting the worst. It was very clear that every step of the way and every job that Gambler had been asked to do in the past had turned into a major hassle for him and he had just had enough of it. What an unbelievable mess for a four-year-old horse to get into. He was a classic case of pressing on with the system regardless of, or oblivious to, the feel.

As we put Carrie on, again Gambler was very apprehensive. When she sat there quietly and asked for nothing, Gambler began to wonder. Carrie asked him forward and I gave him a bit of a lead. It took a few goes before he realized that yes, in fact he could do it on his own and yes, he could get it right. The more things that went right, the easier it became to ask him for new things. In a couple of days we had him going round the sand quite well, but even now he was stopping and locking up, and not coping too well walking past the gate. I knew that he had done a lot more than we were asking of him in his recent past, albeit reluctantly, and I began to see that he needed a bit more focus and direction from his rider. I asked Sarah if she would ride him and with just that bit more experience and clarity of 'ask' he was off without a problem. Stop, start, turn, and little bits of trot. He liked to get it right: we made it easy for him, and he was starting to look very promising. Would Mary still be keen to offload him?

We had gone several days without a hitch and it was time for Mary to take a turn at riding Gambler. We put her up and Gambler looked a bit worried. Mary asked for forward and Gambler didn't move, so Mary tried to push him forwards with her seat and Gambler began to get into a state. These were difficult, difficult moments as so many thoughts and emotions kicked off in everyone at the same time. Mary was feeling awful and I was feeling embarrassed. I could see what was happening – she was just doing far too much and Gambler couldn't handle it – but I find it difficult to say things sometimes. I am not a trained riding instructor and what I know about riding isn't really about technique and style, so whenever I am asked for my opinion on this subject I always feel a bit exposed. In the end I suggested that she sit still and quietly ask for one thing only. At first she couldn't do it: her head was full of all the ideas that people had given her over the years. She was desperately upset because Gambler was upset, and it was all getting a bit tearful. I had to find a way to ask her to abandon everything she had learnt and start again from nothing.

When girls start crying you can spot my style a mile off. It includes lots of reassurance and goes something like this: 'Mary, there's nothing wrong with what you are doing, you're a good rider, you're fine. It's just that right now Gambler needs very clear instructions. You need to do less.' I desperately wanted to ask her to stop moving about but she had been taught that that was what you were supposed to do. She wanted to ride from her seat, which is fair enough – I don't mind how people ride, as long as their horse is happy with it – but what she was doing was confusing Gambler, he needed things simple. So we went right back to basics, and started to work on one cue for one action. We worked on stuff that Gambler understood, because definitely the first priority was not to confuse him.

As it turned out, Mary was quite relieved to be told to sit there and be quiet. If you are a riding expert or a riding teacher, forgive me if you think she should have been doing more, but sometimes it's good to rebuild from the beginning, and I am sure that Mary's riding benefited from a re-evaluation on her part, and it meant Gambler could cope too. Two or three days later Gambler and Mary were hacking around the block, and the most beautiful thing of all was that Gambler was truly more than happy doing it.

And no, I didn't get that horse after all. Just as well really – he was capable of doing far more than I would ever need.

# Give your horse time

Colette is a really small person who, by some strange quirk of fate, has a passion for huge horses. When you see her pick up the back foot of one of her Ardennes or Shire crosses, what you see is this huge foot and vast amounts of feather flying around, and this tiny little person lost in there amongst it all. Every time I work with her, I try to persuade her that it would all be a lot easier if she would settle for a Dartmoor pony, but oh no, 'How could a Dartmoor pony pull a set of harrows, or take us all down the pub in the cart?'

Patch was a really nice, huge piebald gelding. He was originally paired up with a similar horse called Moss, but Moss had to go to make the books balance and that left Patch on his own. Anyway, the books still weren't balancing so Patch had to go too. Colette brought him up to us to see if we could get him a bit more saleable. He can't have been too bad, because I can only remember one thing about him. He was very slow. It was while working with Patch that I first realized how important it is to give your horse time.

I enjoyed working with Patch. He was like a huge old-fashioned machine, in that when you pressed the button you had to wait for something to happen. Even when just leading him around, I had already spotted that it was taking a while for the message to get through. After asking him to move there would be a delay before his feet started to move. It seemed as if that was how long it took – from me getting his attention through his eyes and ears, and then asking through the feel of the rope being lifted and starting to show him a forward movement – for the request to get up to his brain and then all the way along his body and down into his feet, and then for them actually to start to move. The whole thing was taking a good couple of seconds.

Now, if anyone reading this is thinking that that horse just needed sharpening up – well, that's exactly what I thought, and to this day I'm not totally convinced that might not have been the case. But Patch was bred to hoe cabbages, not to do gymkhana, and for that job a bit of slowness would be a positive advantage.

However, the point of this story is that in the time it took for Patch to act on the message, people were understandably getting impatient, and before the message had reached its destination they were firing off another one, and so on until sometimes there would be several messages all at once waiting for processing. You could almost see the steam coming out of Patch's ears. His internal communication system was seizing up in the same way that a computer does when it gets overloaded with junk mail. While his body was trying to react to the first message, his brain was trying to program the next message and then the next message, and Patch, bless his heart, was giving up.

⬤ In some ways, horses are a bit like men. We're fine as long as you only give us one thing to do at a time. Two things and it starts to get tricky and three, we're in trouble. I guess it would be a good study for someone to do to see if male and female horses are the same as male and female humans in this respect. I know from listening to riding instructors teaching that an awful lot of horses have to cope with multi-instructions, and they obviously learn to do just that. But for me that is very advanced stuff: if I can find a way of using one cue for one action, it suits both the horse and me a lot better.

So, up I got on Patch and my aim was to get him moving forward to the cue of a 'kissing' sound. Ultimately, I wanted to be able to get his attention, probably by picking up the reins and letting him feel a bit more energy coming into my body, and then one kiss and off we go. I can tell you, the temptation to boot him was huge, and I did try it now and again, but in the end I realized that a simple cue was the most effective tool. Good communication between Patch and me, with me allowing time for the message to get through, was what worked best. And then I started to see how it was all going to work. As the communication system started to bed down into Patch's tiny brain (and I don't mean that to sound like a put-down, it's just how it looked at the time), as the lines began to clear, Patch's reaction times started to speed up too. Suddenly I had the feeling that this was a job that between us we could do, and I began to get much more enthusiastic.

I don't think Patch will ever be super-quick to react to the cues, but as the saying goes 'horses for courses': some people don't look for those qualities in a horse. The important thing is that when we made things as clear as possible for him, we began to get the best from him. So if you find that your horse isn't responding as you would like, consider the possibility that he may just need a bit of time to think about what you're asking him to do. Of course, I'm not saying that you should wait forever for your horse to get into gear, but sometimes just that bit too much pressure can really slow things up.

# Don't make it hard for your horse

Clarity is a huge part of getting a good result from your horse. Being with horses should not be some kind of grey area where we vaguely attempt to ask for something and the horse vaguely tries to work out what we want. Now that I endeavour to be very conscious of the effect all my actions have on my horse, I can see why horses find some things we do to them amazingly confusing. A question I find myself asking many times when watching some people at work with their horses is 'How the hell is your horse supposed to work out what all that is about?' A good piece of advice is to 'read' the horse. But what does that actually mean? I think it means to be conscious of the effect on the horse of the actions that you are taking. When you start to read the horse, and see the responses to your actions in him, and begin to take these responses into account to determine your further actions, then you will begin to get results.

● I have watched even well-known trainers load a whole heap of demands onto their horses in order to get their message across. Take a look and you will see trainers backing up horses repeatedly, using far more pressure than the horse really needs in order to understand what in fact could be done with a very simple and polite request. You will see people using flailing ropes to send their horses backwards, or you will see horses on the end of ropes going round and round in circles endlessly for no apparent purpose. I can only presume – and I wonder if the trainers realize this – that the purpose of these kinds of actions is to tell the horse that his best bet is to surrender and ask no questions. What it does tell the horse is that this person is an irrational being who communicates in an alien way, and one with whom he cannot communicate back. People who persist in going down these roads run the risk of making what can be a relatively simple job of creating a trusting communication far more difficult.

A while back I did some work in a showing yard. They had a pony that was supposedly 'bored' with showing, and was 'being naughty' about standing up for the judge. He just wouldn't stand still in the correct position and, in the owner's words, 'He definitely knows what he is supposed to be doing because he has been doing it for years.' I asked the owner to show me the problem, and my heart sank when I saw what was happening. The pony was getting so many cues he didn't know what to do. He was pushed, pulled, pinched in the chest, and had it explained to him in clear English exactly how he should be standing. In the end he just gave up trying and then he got a slap and a bit of verbal, realized he had better carry on trying to find what it was that the owner wanted, tried again for a while and then gave up again.

I do sometimes wonder if I am a bit out of touch with what the competitive owner wants from their horse, but in this case I think my horror was justified. All my instincts were telling me to get out of the yard as quickly as possible, so I started searching round for a way of explaining that I was not very experienced at showing and maybe it would be a good idea to get someone in who knew more about these kind of problems. Alas, I hadn't accounted for the presence of my dear wife, who barged into the arena and started vigorously questioning this quite formidable lady about exactly what *was* her cue for this pony to stand correctly? Anyone who knows me will no doubt have a very clear picture in their mind of me wilting into the background as I watched this 'clash of the titans' unfolding in front of me. I could see no way out. It was like watching a terrier trying to get a bone off a rottweiler. Let's just say that there wasn't a lot of give from either side.

But, credit where it's due, from out of this chaos came a solution, a lesson was learnt by everyone present, and the pony was grateful too. In the end, in a desperate attempt to find a way through, I took the pony and asked the lady exactly what it was she wanted. She said she needed the pony's leg a bit further forward but with him not just pointing his toe, he had to be putting his weight on it. I gently asked him forward using the slightest cue on the reins, and when he had got it just right I released the cue and leaned forward towards him so you could hardly see me doing it. He stopped and I took all the pressure off him by taking my focus elsewhere – he knew he had got it right. The owner then walked round to the other side. This time the pony had to back up a step and pose the same way but from the other side. I moved gently into him and he just did it dead right. Was it a fluke? We did it a few times without a problem and then the owner had a go. No problems there and everyone was feeling good. I was grateful to Sarah for not letting me slink off out of a difficult situation. She was chuffed because she was right about the problem. And the owner was chuffed because she could get what she wanted from the pony. And the pony, who was previously accused of looking 'dead' and 'switched off', was looking really good because he knew how to do what his handler was asking him to do.

So often we just do too much too quickly. The horse becomes confused by us, and ends up getting the blame. That's not really good enough, is it?

# Stay ahead of the game

I once owned a horse called Prudence. I wish I had never sold her, because she was the second most comfortable horse I've ever ridden. I am so annoyed about it every time I think about it, but anyway I sold her.

The first person to come and see her was a guy about my age who told us he could ride fine, but afterwards admitted he was a complete beginner. So we tacked up Prudence and the rider got on and set off down the drive. Just before the road there was an open field gate on his left. Prudence saw the gate and decided that she was going through it. She got into the field and trotted off down the bank, and the rider, in slow motion, slid around her body and hit the deck. Amazingly, he still tried to buy the horse off me, but by then I was beginning to realize that he maybe wasn't quite up to the job. So what happened there? At the time I just put it down to complete lack of experience and thought no more about it.

A couple of days later a young girl came along to try out the horse. I guess if I had been a sharp horse dealer I would have shut the gate, but I didn't, and blow me if Prudence didn't do the same thing again. This time the girl did at least stay on, and by the time she had got to the bottom of the field, she had gathered herself together and managed to get Prudence back up to the lane, no problem.

This all happened quite a long time ago, but it was a big lesson for me for several reasons. The first thing that amazed me was the fact that this wasn't happening to me, so I could watch myself to see what I was doing. I was pleased to find I was, in fact, just that tiny little bit ahead of the game. I could feel Prudence thinking in advance of her action and so I just let her know that no, we're not going that way, we are going to walk straight past that open gate. Now I know that pretty much everyone who reads this book would have got past that open gate just fine, but would you all have been able to work out how or why you did it? It's all about giving your horse time and keeping up with or ahead of her thought processes. If you give her time to take on board the information that you are *going straight on*, then the problem doesn't arise. If you leave it until she has decided otherwise, then you will most definitely have to deal with the problem. I like watching good riders and good horsemen because they tend to be just one step ahead of the game. In the case of Prudence and the gateway, what you would have to do would be so small that most people would not be able to see you do it, but the result of your actions would be huge. Just a tiny touch on the rein about three metres before the gate, or even better just as you felt Prudence's focus wander through it, was all that would be needed to get her focus up ahead again instead of through the gate.

If you can't, or don't, read your horse, you will miss your opportunity, and that is what 'be with your horse' is all about. If you are not with your horse, can you really expect your horse to be with you?

Another important aspect of giving your horse time showed up in the loading job with Ruth and Martin that I talked about earlier. When Martin asked Soldier forward, and the horse gave him forward, Martin correctly gave him the release. At this point Soldier needed time to appreciate that he had got something right. A quick release quickly followed by another ask, was too much for the horse – he couldn't separate the two signals. But when he came forward and got his release and was given time to appreciate it, he was actually leaning forward looking for more. Again, success came from reading the horse and being there with him, feeling what he was feeling – not from blindly acting out some formulaic method from a text book.

## More about giving your horse time

And then, of course, there is the whole other meaning of 'give your horse time', and that is all about being patient and playing what poker players call 'a long game'. One of the most enjoyable things about life is that when you practise something you get better at it. Seeing that improvement come over days, weeks, months and years can be a source of great satisfaction, but to do that you have to have the vision to look back to where you once were and see the journey that you have already made. I do this a lot with people if they get a little despondent that things aren't working out for them with one particular task. I ask them to remember back to what things were like when we first started on the job and get the picture of long-term progress, rather than focusing on what may seem a little bit rough right now.

I think it's fine to be a perfectionist, but perfection has to be aimed for over time. 'It'll come' is one of my favourite expressions, but I'm not sure that perfection, at least in this material world, ever does. Going back again to Martin and Ruth's loading problem, I saw pretty early on that Soldier was not at all happy with coming out of the trailer, so that became my main priority and my next job. For some reason, when he got to a certain point in backing out of the trailer, he became very anxious, threw his head in the air and rushed backwards very quickly. We needed to show him that he didn't need to worry at this point or, to put it another way, he needed to practise his backing out until he was confident enough to do it without any anxiety.

We were starting from a point where backing out was a major problem, even to the extent that I would say it was probably the main reason that Soldier was unsure about the wisdom of going into the trailer in the first place. So we began our practice session with one step onto the ramp and then backing that one step off the ramp. We built this up until he was quite happy backing down the ramp from halfway into the trailer, which was just about the point where he had been panicking in the first place. I wouldn't say he was really good at this at this stage, but he was getting better as we went along, and so were we. By the time we were ready for a coffee break, we had the big horse walking in and backing out with maybe a bit of anxiety now and again at the crucial point but nothing like how it had been when we first started. He took his break knowing that he could at least do the job, which was good progress whichever way you look at it. By the way, we hadn't been working for long by this point, maybe half an hour, but that was with other things thrown in too. I'm not too keen on boring boring boring, work work work. Maybe I'm humanizing my horses here, but I like to think that they prefer things fresh and so I avoid just drilling them over and over on one similar task.

After coffee we had another go and the big horse backed out of that trailer as if he had been doing it all his life. That time he probably scored seven out of ten for it, so there was still room for improvement, but hey, give him time, he'll get there. We went in and out of the trailer just once in that second session and then we put him away. He'd got that, and I felt that tomorrow he'd probably score eight, no problem. He's not so worried about backing out; he's not so worried about going in either. He's not perfect yet, but give it time... it'll come!

# Get your horse's attention

One important point that is linked very closely to giving your horse time is the art of getting your horse's attention. This is a real common sense thing that I've noticed good horsemen do all the time, some of them probably without even realizing. Every time you ask for your horse's attention, and you get that attention, is one more time that the horse has acknowledged that you are in charge. As with a lot of small things to do with horses, the implications of doing it or not doing it can be huge.

I use 'getting the attention' as a big part of setting up the relationship between the horse and me. The first time I meet a new horse, when I set out to show him that I need my personal space and that I am in control of the movement, I also ask him to give me his attention. What I am after is not to have the horse fixated on me in some kind of intense way – I just want him to be there with me, and not fixated on something else. This is the default situation I want to be in with my horse. It means that if I want to ask him to do something, then I can easily get his attention, usually with a kissing noise (once, in his direction), at which point he realizes that I am about to ask for something; then, when I ask, he is ready to do it, and off we go.

● I want to get my horse to this point in the most gentle way that I can, and the reason for doing this gently is not just because I want everything to be gentle and nice and so on, it's because gentle works better. Say you have your horse on a lead rope and his attention wanders away from you and over the hedge, if you gently ask him back to you he will more than likely just come back. If you pull too hard on the rope you will more than likely get the opposite reaction, where he will pull against you. If you do get him to come back to you through excessive force, OK you got a result, but it could be a result with a price. With gentle comes respect – with rough comes fear.

On a practical level, it is a very good idea to get into the habit of getting the horse's attention before asking him to do something for you. For example, sometimes you can clearly see someone ask their horse to move forward when being ridden. In this instance let's say the cue they choose to use is nudging their heels onto the horse's flanks. However, at the same time as the cue is used, the horse's attention happens to be 'away with the fairies' over on the other side of the yard, so the first thing he knows about moving off is the heels into his flanks. It's all come as a bit of a surprise and he wasn't really ready to go, so he starts to get organized... and then the rider asks again with a bit more urgency. This time the horse gets going, so everything is fine. It's all happened a bit quickly and he's not quite sure where he's going, but he's on his way and the rider is happy. But it's not fine really, is it? Because now the horse thinks that the first ask was to get him ready and the second was for walk, so from now on it's going to take two kicks, the second one harder than the first, to get the horse going. How much tidier would it be, and how much better would it feel, to have your horse there ready on standby? Get his attention with a small cue like a kiss or maybe by lifting the reins very slightly, then use your cue for move off which could be sitting up a bit, getting a bit of energy into your body and focusing up ahead, and away you go.

A similar situation quite often arises when horses are being led. The handler just walks off, and the horse happens to be looking the other way, so the first thing he knows about it is when the rope nearly pulls his head off. It's not comfortable for the horse or the handler, as they both come to terms with all the conflicting energies of horse's head and handler's arms going in different directions. So much better to have your horse there ready, let him know that you are about to move, set off and have him follow you. No tension in the rope, no sudden jagging, just one smooth flow.

All this may seem to be such obvious stuff, but it is stuff that sometimes gets missed and can often cause misunderstandings that lead to bigger issues later on. Think about poor old Patch, the massive piebald cob: he had a two-second delay between the cue being given and the action beginning in his feet, and that two-second delay was assuming he was ready in the first place. What was it like for him when he wasn't ready at all? He was being kicked about four or five times before he even began to move, and all this was contributing to a mass of confusion that made everything even harder for him. As soon as the cues were organized and simplified, then he could start to work on improving his reaction times, which is exactly what he did.

# Be clear, and be sure you're being clear

As I go around the countryside working with horses, I feel very lucky in that I have the opportunity to learn from every job. I get to see a lot of different situations that people are in with their horses. I do sometimes feel a bit of a fraud, because I am able to work with some very good and knowledgeable horse people, and truly I do not know a huge amount about the 'horse world', but what I do know is that just by making things a bit simpler, very often problems can be sorted out. This is why I feel justified in writing about the simple approach – because sometimes, in the great scheme of things, we forget the simplicity, and in the drive to achieve our goals, we tend to gloss over the small things that are going wrong, and those small things can often turn into bigger things... and then the problems begin.

● Sometimes just a few small changes in the way that you are with your horse can make all the difference. It is important to realize that it is how you are that determines how your horse is. You are key to the whole thing. There is no magic switch that will make everything work, nor any piece of equipment that will sort it all out for you. The horse needs you to be there for him, and thankfully that in itself is not a difficult responsibility for you to fulfil.

Number one priority on your list is to be clear in what you are asking for. You also need to have a clear way of letting your horse know that he has understood and done (or at least made an attempt to do) what you are asking for. Horses do not appreciate grey areas: they feel that these have to be clarified and lack of clarification causes them anxiety. Horses like everything to be presented to them in very black-and-white terms – that is when they begin to relax. Again, this is such a simple thing and it is so easy to get it right; yet it is also so easy to get it wrong, and the consequences of getting it wrong can be huge.

Think back for a moment to the subject of personal space. For many people, and their horses, there is no clear line drawn on this issue, and this can be a major factor in the inability of the horse to relax. If the horse is unsure about something, he will question the situation to try to clear up the uncertainty. On the issue of personal space, he will ask you, 'Where is the line?'. Until you tell him where it is, he will move further and further into your space until you *have* to tell him for your own safety. By this point you will probably have quite a pushy horse on your hands who, quite rightly, is beginning to think that he is in charge. How much easier for both of you if you had just used this simple issue to demonstrate early on where the boundaries are.

If you keep things clear and simple, you will stack the odds in favour of getting it right – you can do the complicated stuff later if you still want to, but the likelihood is that you will find a simpler way through on that too. When you and your horse are ready to do the complicated stuff, it won't be complicated.

## Don't nag your horse

Be careful not to fall into the trap of nagging your horse. This is a real danger if you do something just enough to annoy the horse but not enough to achieve a lasting result. I watched one owner work with her horse for a whole summer, and a few times I explained to her that when you have to correct something over and over it really shows that you are not getting it right. In this case, the horse kept moving into her whenever she was working around him. She could be grooming him, putting a saddle on him or putting on his bridle, and all the time he would want to be 'in her face'. So I said to her, 'Why don't you draw a line at the distance that you want him to be from you, stick to it, and he will stop crowding you out like that?'

The lady had watched me work once or twice and at that time I was using a hissing noise quite a lot to get horses to give me some space. So, fair enough, that's what she started doing too. The problem was that she made the noise and the horse moved back a bit, but within seconds he returned. So she made the noise again and the same thing happened all over again. Amazingly, this happened all summer, so whenever you were around these two there was this constant ineffective hissing noise going on. For the horse, the sound had become no more than slightly irritating background music.

Take a leaf out of Sarah's book. If she wants me to do something, she'll maybe ask me a couple of times, but if I don't take any notice she starts to lose the plot completely. Now, I don't want to be around that, do I? So as soon as I see even the start of it, I'm off and running to get the job done. That's how you have to be with your horse – your action has to *mean* something or it's better not done at all. Once your horse knows you mean business, then you won't need to go down that road. Again, read the horse and use what is necessary to get to where you both need to be.

## Spot the real problem

It was going to be a really hot day. As I walked up to the yard, the sun was shining through the trees and I felt privileged to be alive.

I had taken a phone call half an hour before from a lady down the road whose horse wouldn't stand still for the farrier. He was in the 'last chance saloon'. If he didn't get it right the next time, the owner was going to have to find a new farrier; and this is not an easy task around here. From the yard I could hear the horse coming up the road and I wondered what I was going to do to help out with this problem. There's nothing worse than seeing horses wheeling around on three legs with a farrier hanging on in there trying to get the job done. It is one of those situations that only ever seems to get worse. I was wondering how I could avoid going down the same road.

James and his owner hadn't been in the yard more than about a minute before I could see work that needed to be done. He was a

*'There's nothing worse than seeing horses wheeling around on three legs
with a farrier hanging on in there trying to get the job done.'*

beautiful four-year-old Dales pony and his owner was a really kind, well-meaning and well-educated lady who knew a lot about her horses. However, what I could see was that there was so much going on that there wasn't even a moment when nothing was happening. Never mind standing still for the farrier: the horse couldn't stand still for anything. So from there the job was easy. We needed to show James how to stand still and put this stillness on cue, then when the farrier arrived we could just cue up the horse and away he could go to get those shoes on.

I took the horse and showed him my personal boundaries. That cut out all the movements towards and around me, so then he switched his attention to things away from me. I spent a few minutes gently asking him to come back to me every time his attention wandered off, rewarding him by standing quietly with him whenever he got it right, and it didn't take too long before we had a little bit of quiet to work with. The thing is, if you don't establish 'a little bit of quiet', or what I call 'nothing', then the horse's attention always has to be somewhere else. It is very handy to show the horse that he can actually relax – that he can just stand there and rely on you to take care of things. With some horses, it is almost as if they have forgotten how to do nothing, and in a lot of cases this is simply because their owners just do too much. They never give their horses a moment when nothing is happening – they're either grooming them, or talking to them, or looking at them. There is just so much attention, and if and when it all stops the horse simply starts to look for more. The horse turns into an attention junkie, and that can be a complete nightmare.

So, we quickly got to half a minute or so of just standing there, and as the old saying goes, 'if you can get one minute then you can get two', and that is exactly how we did it. Interestingly, it was almost harder work to get the same result with the owner than it was with the horse – and that says it all, doesn't it?

Anyway, by the time the farrier came up a few days later, we were very well prepared and things didn't go too badly. It's not so easy for a young horse to stand on three legs for a long period of time, nor is it such a good idea for young horses to think farriers are a hassle, so a bit of quick shoeing isn't a bad idea for the first few times. James's farrier did a fantastic job in terms of the shoeing itself, but it all took a bit too long, especially for a young horse who found standing still a bit of a trial. I found myself thinking that we should have sacrificed a bit of the quality in the shoeing to get the job done a little more quickly.

# Understand the principles

I have already said that I don't like systems, and yet I have to admit that I have already told you about more than one 'system' I use myself. It would be extremely difficult to work with horses without any system at all. Imagine walking into the stable with absolutely no preconceived idea of what you were going to do – that sounds a bit like I used to be with my horses about 15 years ago.

● What I want to get across in this book, and what I believe is the key to success with horses, is an understanding of the *principles behind the systems*. Working with horses is not just a series of actions that guarantee a result. It is very important to understand that it is not a good idea to have a system that says: when the horse does this, do that, and when it does that, do this! We are working with living creatures here, not machines. Horses respond differently to different situations and to different pressures of ask – one thing may send a particular horse into orbit, while another horse may not even notice it. You have to read the situation and be with each different horse in each different moment.

I recently read a long correspondence about how to deal with a bitey horse. Some people were saying that a swift blow in the mouth as the horse bit would do the trick, others that a gentle kick on the leg would distract it from biting. And I was thinking, well, why is this horse biting, can't we get at that and sort that out? This is what I mean about principles – I know sometimes we have to treat the symptoms, but it is so much better if we can address the cause. Does that horse go around biting all the other horses he meets? Of course he doesn't. Maybe he will bite one or two of them, but probably not. The horse is biting because the relationship between the handler and the horse is set up that way.

So when someone tells you their little trick for dealing with a bitey horse, just remember that that is what it is – a little trick. It doesn't cure the underlying problem of why the horse was biting you in the first place. And that is the job you really need to be working on.

Sometimes this can be a really difficult stance to take. Let's go back again to bad loaders – they are such good examples. I once ended up in a fairly unfriendly yard trying to load a big, frightened horse into a lorry. This horse couldn't even lead up the lane without a struggle, let alone lead into the back of a lorry. Even trying to lead him into his stable was a major job. I realized that I was in a vulnerable situation in terms of success and failure, but I stuck to my guns and said my piece. I explained that the horse was nowhere near being ready to load into a lorry when he couldn't even lead across the yard. 'We've got the wrong guy here!' was writ large on the faces of the assembled throng.

If only I'd had the nerve to walk away then, but I didn't. I tried for two hours to set up some kind of relationship between that horse and me so that we could at least lead over a pole or two, but he wasn't interested. He was rearing and charging about on the end of the rope in response to the simplest of asks. I never got anywhere near working with the lorry – there was simply no point. The horse needed a lot more time and a lot more help to change his ideas about humans and what they were about.

I left that yard exhausted and depressed, and I later heard that one of the people watching that day had described me as 'absolute rubbish'. It takes time for me to come to terms with that kind of experience: how far away from mine are those people's ideas about horses? But the days go by and the dust settles, and I always end up back at the same place – thankfully, not back at that yard, I mean the same place within myself. The answer is always the same: I have to get back to the principles – get things right between the horse and me, and then work from there.

You know, the thing is you can't change yourself, well not all at once anyway. You have to work from where you are in the moment that you are doing what you are doing. You will change from day to day, but not hugely. So when things go a bit wrong and you get thrown a little off course, don't worry too much. You are who you are and you'll be back before too long.

## Gentle – all the time?

So far I have put a lot of emphasis on the need to be gentle in the way you work with your horse. But let's get real: sometimes it just isn't like that, is it? I agree that sometimes things do get a bit hectic, and I don't have a problem with that. However, my view is that if you offer gentle first, then most horses will go with that and be gentle with you. I often find that it is possible to do an entire session with a difficult horse that I have never seen before, without using much more than a very gentle approach throughout.

Horses are very sensitive to pressure, to such an extent that if you are really sensitive to their reactions it is very often possible to find a level to work at that genuinely does not need to go beyond the gentle. Sometimes, of course, it is not so easy, and then, as far as I can, I leave it to the horse to choose if he wants to work at a more physical level. A good example of this would be if I was working with a horse and he suddenly decided that he wanted to spin around and run off. The first thing to look at is whether I gave him a good reason to run off, and I have to be confident that I didn't. I definitely try to work below the threshold that would cause any fear, let alone panic, in the horse, but sometimes it doesn't work out. Of course, in the horse's mind he must have had a good reason to run off, otherwise he wouldn't have done it. In this case, my aim is to show him, in one way or another, that there is a better reason for staying than for running off.

I don't consider myself to be someone who puts unreasonable demands on horses, but sometimes it may take a bit of time for a horse to work that out. Sometimes I feel I need the horse to give me that time when he would prefer otherwise. I know some people will be uncomfortable that I seem to be imposing my will on the horse in this way – but each individual person has to reach their own decisions in each moment as things happen with their horses. Sometimes I do take the decision that I need to push things on faster than maybe the horse thinks is a good idea.

● **Horses are very compromised by their situation with humans: no matter how we look at it, we are imposing our will on them. Sometimes, when a horse strongly contests this it is better to get it sorted out quickly rather than go through a huge lengthy debate with him about the whole thing. If a horse chooses to barge through me, I will do whatever it takes to show him that it is not such a good idea and he needs to back off. I will do as little as possible to achieve this retreat, but I will also do virtually anything to achieve it too. I genuinely feel that if I am not prepared to do this, then I should leave that horse alone and not be**

**meddling with him in the first place. I strongly believe that it is extremely unfair to the horse to expect him to work with you, but then not give him guidelines – that he clearly understands – to work within.**

Some time ago I was in a field with an owner and her two horses. It was very windy and she had already tried to bring one of the horses into the yard and he had broken away from her and run off. This time we thought it might be better to bring the two horses in together, so we got hold of them both at the same time. Before we had walked more than a couple of metres, a gust of wind blew up and the horse the owner was holding took off. She didn't stand a chance and had to let him go. He charged across the field. The horse I was holding reared up, wheeled around and took off, but in that split second I made a different plan and tried to hold on to him.

He was not a small horse, but when he hit the end of the rope somehow I managed to hold him. He regrouped and had another go, and a couple more after that, and as luck would have it each time I managed to hang on to him. He needed to think then, so he stopped for a second or two to reassess his options. I stood quietly while he thought about it, and after a few seconds I gently asked him to move forwards. He took a couple of steps and tried to run off again, but by now he was beginning to realize that getting away was not an automatic option. We stood quietly again for a few seconds and then moved on. We got back to the stables in one piece and after a coffee (he had hay), we got down to some serious horse work.

Looking back, what were my options? Ideally, I would rather not have ended up in that situation, but I did. I would have dearly loved to have had a few warm, sunny days with no wind over which to build up such a good relationship with the horse that the thought of running off wouldn't even enter his head. I was on such a potential loser in all that wind that maybe I should have let the horse go on his first try, because I knew that with each subsequent try the stakes for me became even higher. I really didn't need him to know that he could get away from me by using such forceful behaviour. I know I got lucky with that one, and I also know I should try not to get into that kind of thing in the first place, but that is what happened and how I dealt with it at the time. I used force, but I didn't pull the horse, he pulled me – I just stood there.

The amazing thing was that as soon as the horse realized the consequences of pulling, he was able to see the advantage of not doing it, relax and concentrate on the job in hand. This, for me, is the dichotomy of working with horses: I want them to have freedom in terms of choice, but it is important that that choice does not lead to doubt. Horses do not thrive with doubt in their minds.

• • •

Two horse trainers had a bet. They each had an untouched foal and the bet was to see who had the best-trained foal after four days. One of the trainers decided that they would use no force and would progress only at a speed the foal was happy with, and the other trainer decided that they would push things on if and when necessary.

Within two hours, the second trainer had lassoed the foal, put a halter on and started working on leading. The other trainer spent the first three days trying to show his pony that he was no threat and that having a halter on was not a problem at all. So, which was the happier pony – the one who went through 15 minutes of concern at the beginning and then quickly realized that things were all right after all, or the one who spent three days worrying and trying to work out if he really should trust the person or not?

OK, both the foals ended up happy to be with their handlers but, economics aside, I'm sure the second one had the easier time – and the trainer had three extra days to get on to other things. I'm not giving my vote to violent and aggressive handling, or doing things just for the sake of speed, but there are some circumstances where I think it is best to crack on a little bit for the sake of the horse. I can't imagine that either trainer damaged either foal in this story, but prolonged uncertainty for a horse can easily lead to a state of anxiety about humans that could turn into a real problem. If I see something I am doing with a horse is going nowhere fast, I like to look for a way out for both of us. Sometimes bashing on in the same way when things aren't working out can take everything in a backward direction – be careful not to dig deeper holes.

## Keep your horse conscious

When we use methods of training that initiate the flight instinct in the horse, one thing we need to consider is that we are showing him, to some degree, that we have the power to engender fear. I'm not saying that this is necessarily a bad thing – it isn't hard to imagine that there are some circumstances in which a little bit of fear can be quite useful. (I once had to drive a stallion away from a mare, who he was mercilessly beating up. That day I did need to use some fear.) What I am saying is that *you have to make a choice* about how much power you want to use, or at least how much of the fear factor you want to introduce to the horses with which you are working.

I have found that by keeping the horse conscious – that is, by working at a level where he is not afraid and is therefore able to think – it is often possible to establish a good working relationship quite quickly. At one of our workshops, a lady came along with a ten-year-old thoroughbred mare with which she was having a lot of difficulties. The horse was fine to ride but she was not so much fun to handle when you were on the ground, and when she was being lunged she just took off and ran. I know it is not a good idea to pigeonhole people, but we all do it and I did it to this owner – I saw her as a real regular horsewoman who had somehow missed out on all the so-called 'alternative' stuff that has been around for the last few years. Annie was at her wits' end with this little mare who just couldn't get anything right in the yard.

I watched the two of them together for a while and there was no communication going on at all. Actually, the truth is that there was lots of communication going on, but it was all utterly chaotic and totally unhelpful. The mare was very sensitive indeed and was reacting to *everything* the owner was doing. The owner, for her part, was doing far too much that didn't come across to the horse as being of any positive help, and between them they were getting into a real mess.

Sometimes these really sensitive horses can be very difficult to work with because of their apparent over-reaction to what you are doing. But once you realize that the actions of the horse are a response to your actions and you then tailor your input accordingly, the possibilities really begin to open up. This mare proved to be ideal for showing the owner exactly how she needed to be in order to get the most from her horse.

You really do not want this kind of horse flying away from you in fear, and that would have been oh so easy to achieve. The idea that force of any kind would be helpful in this case is ludicrous. What the mare needed was some good, conscious work. She needed to see that we humans make sense. I think this is the way to be with all horses, by the way, but with some it's more obvious than with others.

I took the mare into the round pen and led her around on a loose rope. She was a joy for me to lead, but she had to have a loose rope – she didn't need the input from a tight hold, that's for sure. I wanted to show her that I was in charge of the movement and the speed but I didn't want to send her into orbit. I let her off the rope and asked her to move slowly in walk around the pen. She found this quite difficult and wanted to run, but I just asked her quietly to come back to walk and to keep walking. In this situation, it is all about the energy you put into it. You have to be like a tap that turns the energy up and down according to the response you get from the horse – that is communication. Once you get that, and your horse gets that you get it, you are on your way.

As soon as the little mare saw that I was with her she really began to relax, and before long we were doing nice controlled turns and then adding in a few steps of trot and coming nicely back to walk. I love this kind of work because it is real communication. For me it is the beginning of the horse learning to be with the human, and I mean *be with* the human – you know, really *with* them, every second of the way. Right the way through this, I strive to keep the horse conscious. If the mare lost the plot and ran off into instinct mode, I worked to bring her back. I wanted her with me.

Then came lunging. I clipped on the rope and, using the same ideas, asked the mare to walk around me in a circle. It didn't take long for her to work out what I was after. As far as she was concerned, the difference between stop and walk was for me to go from being soft with my eyes on the ground to being slightly more energetic with my eyes on her shoulder. Off she would go, and to stop her I would virtually have to die on the spot, but she got it and it worked well. To go from walk to trot, I moved my eyes from her shoulder onto her eye and put a tad more life in my body.

● When I'm working on walk to trot I often like to ask for just a few steps of trot at first and then back to walk to make sure all the cues are set up. I want everything happening on cue and working as a partnership, not the horse running away from me in fear. I want the horse to feel every step of the way. Once I've got things working pretty well in a small way, then I'll ask for more. It's automatic if the system is set up and the horse understands it, and it's chaos if she doesn't. Because I so clearly remember in my early days with horses being giving instructions that I didn't understand, and how desperate it was for me trying to implement those instructions, I am careful to try not to do exactly the same thing to the horse.

So now it was Annie's turn. Never before had she even imagined that her horse was a reflection of how she was behaving, so she was going through a steep learning curve on that one alone. Combine that with quite a lot of guilt about what her horse had been putting up with for the last few years and she was getting a bit emotional. Now, I'm not a supporter of guilt, so I got her in the pen as quickly as possible to prove to her that she could do it too.

Sometimes things just go your way and this was one of those times. Annie picked it up like a dream and for the first time in years she and her horse were literally dancing together, first loose and then on the rope. At the end of the session they had a big cuddle and that was a first too, so we all went home happy that day!

This is not to say that all Annie's problems were over – of course not. But she went home with her horse knowing that good things were possible, and that there is more to keeping horses than just wandering around in a confused daze. She had things to work on and I felt confident that with a bit of effort she could turn their relationship around. Be conscious of the effect you are having and maybe your horse will be conscious too!

• • •

Now, about that oft-maligned piece of equipment – the round pen. Come on folks, it's not the tool, it's the way you use it. Let's finally nail that one, shall we? A round pen provides a safe enclosed environment in which to work the horse. I find it really useful because it helps to keep the horse's attention on the job. Also, for starting young horses, it allows the handler to work the horse loose, to establish forward movement, turning and stopping cues before putting the rider up. It is true that it is also a piece of equipment that can be used badly, but this applies to any equipment, doesn't it? The round pen does put the handler in a very powerful position, because the horse cannot run away. Personally, I would not be looking to do anything that would encourage the horse to run away anyway.

# Beyond understanding

People who understand everything worry me a lot. People who speak with conviction about worldly matters worry me even more. I've never really believed that we are equipped to understand everything that's going on here, or that we're supposed to understand it either. So when people say they do understand things, my feeling tends to be that they are either bluffing or suffering from some kind of delusion.

The other day, someone on the radio was saying that there are millions of galaxies out there, and there is a black hole in every galaxy, and the nearest black hole is some 37 million light years from us here on earth. How glad I am I found that out, and now that I've shared it with you, you know it too. What does it actually mean, though? I really didn't have the slightest clue as to what the guy was on about, but he was talking in such an authoritative way that the whole feeling was, 'Well, if you don't understand this you must be a bit stupid.' Even the radio presenter appeared to understand it all too. Please don't ever let me fall into the trap of thinking I know more than anyone else. We might each know a little bit of this and a little bit of that, and I might know my version of how I think things are, but that's all it is: my version, full stop.

So, bearing in mind the possibility that you don't know everything, let me tell you a story about a little mare called Constance. She was a lovely horse that I was trying to sell for a friend of mine and she had a few issues that I wanted to get sorted before she found a new home. One of the first things anyone looking to buy Constance would see was that every time she went from walk to trot she threw her head in the air and kept it there. When I first saw her do it I thought, 'Oh, that will be quite easy to sort out. I'll just show her that she doesn't need to worry about that and then she will relax.' But it wasn't as easy as that.

I asked Carrie to ride Constance around the school in walk and then to speed it up gradually; then, when it felt as if the horse wanted to fall into trot, just let her move on into it. No pressure, no over-asking, just a really nice flow. I'd done this before with a horse that bucked when he went into canter from trot and it had worked a treat. Once the horse realized that he could do this just fine, he never thought to buck again... actually, that's not completely true, he did revert later, but not with my rider. That was a really sensitive horse and the owner couldn't judge the ask. She was simply asking for too much and that's exactly what she got.

Anyway, my 'trick' didn't work with Constance and I know it wasn't Carrie – she knew exactly what I was on about and got it just right. After several tries I decided it wasn't going to happen and that it was time to go back a couple of steps. I wanted to see if I could get Constance to go from walk to trot on a lead rope without a rider on board. Now, I think I'm pretty good at leading horses, and showing a horse that there is absolutely no problem in going from walk to trot is something at which I am very confident. But could I do it this time? It took quite a few tries before I could even get anything remotely relaxed from Constance.

The point of this story is that for me it was an exercise in consciousness. Every time Constance went into trot she panicked and went into flight mode. She was totally unable to relax and make the transition in a conscious state. I believed that once she realized that it wasn't a problem, then she could begin to work on doing it without fear. That is what we were after, and as far as I was concerned, until we were able to help her through that, there was absolutely no point in pushing on with the job. I wouldn't mind betting that the problem happened in the first place due to a combination of an ill-fitting saddle and someone inadvertently pushing the horse on to do something before she was really ready to do it. For Constance, the whole procedure had become enveloped in fear.

Constance was a ten-year-old horse and this problem was in very deep. I would actually describe her as a remedial in the sense that there was no quick fix – not that I could find anyway. I worked on through from the lead rope, onto long lines and it took a couple of weeks to get her just about right. Then we put the rider back on and it all fell apart again, but this time we did get through to her, and more and more as the days passed she began to see that walk to trot was not something to run away from – in fact, it was not difficult at all.

Whenever I meet a new horse that 'has a problem', almost always I look to find that point when fear takes over from conscious work. That is the point where the work can really begin to make a difference. It is in the fear that small problems grow and sometimes turn into insurmountable issues for both horse and owner. Obviously, it is far better not to go down that road in the beginning if it can be avoided.

# Getting into work mode

For centuries, horses have been used by man to work. By discarding the least suitable ones and breeding from the most suitable, through the generations man has selected those horses that most fulfil his needs. Now we have an animal with a very strong work ethic instilled into its DNA. I'm not a scientist, so maybe this is not quite factually correct, but that is what it feels like when I work with horses.

Tiger was a three-year-old thoroughbred filly whose owner Teresa was beginning to find her a bit of a handful. Tiger was fine as long as she was doing what she wanted to do, and was going where she wanted to go, but as soon as Teresa's agenda required something different Tiger couldn't cope with it. Her first answer to everything that she didn't want to do was to rear. Quite often, rearing is way down the line in a horse's list of evasion tactics, giving the owner or handler some time to sort things out well before the situation becomes this dangerous. But Tiger didn't give you a second. If she wanted to go the other way there was no time to persuade her otherwise – she just went up!

I always try to remember to put on my hard hat when I'm working with horses, whatever the situation. Sometimes I forget, but I didn't need reminding with this one. And, as Teresa had predicted, it wasn't long before Tiger was trying big time to go the opposite way to me – and all I had done was to quietly ask her to lead in a small circle in the paddock.

I did a couple of sessions with Tiger, just trying to show her that my agenda wasn't all bad and that in fact it could be really good. I started off in the stable asking for a backward step and built up to leading her around the yard with a bit of sideways and backwards thrown in. We, that's me and Tiger, made good progress and on the third session we, that's me and Teresa, decided that we should all head off up the road to the nearest sand school.

Now, one thing we surely all realize is that when you work with horses anything might happen. We can all play the percentages to try to get things right, but horses are horses and this world is this world, and in the end we are not in control. If you want to be in control there must be plenty of other hobbies or jobs you can get involved in – sometimes I wish I had opted to stick with my childhood interests of stamp collecting and trainspotting. Alas, my desire for street cred led me away from the relative safety of those hobbies into the anarchic chaos that was going on at the time (it was the sixties). Oh what fun we had, or most of us anyway.

Back to earth, and here I was walking up a narrow road with high banks on both sides and Tiger on the end of a rope. Then along came something that had never happened to me before: a herd of bullocks charging down the road towards us, chased along at a fair old speed by a farmer in his Landrover. Quick thinking was absolutely imperative, because there was no way those cows were going to stop. Luckily, there was a gateway that we just managed to swing into as they charged past. Tiger's eyes were out on stalks and I was playing 'Mr Calm' as hard as I could go. Just at the last second Tiger lost the plot and reared. She swung round, landed and looked around, at which point I thought the best course of action would be to move on without too much delay.

We made it to the sand school and I set about trying to bring some order into my relationship with this very edgy young horse. Things were going fine, but the real turning point in the whole session came when I asked Teresa to put out a few poles for us to walk over. Suddenly, the horse changed before our eyes. She had a job, something to do that she understood and that made sense to her, and her whole demeanour was transformed. What a few seconds before had been an anxious, unruly youngster became a beautifully soft, controlled and relaxed potential competition horse. It was a defining moment for the horse and her owner.

Tiger had never stepped over poles before or even seen anything like it, but it really looked as if we had tapped into something within her that she already knew about. That's what I mean when I say it's in the DNA: it really looks as if the horse understands and thrives on the concept of work. I know I had already begun the job

'The real turning point in the whole session came when I asked Teresa to put out a few poles for us to walk over. Suddenly, the horse changed before our eyes. She had something to do that made sense to her, and her whole demeanour was transformed.'

of showing Tiger how things work out between horse and human, but providing the poles as a job for her to do became a great catalyst to spur things on. Obviously the jobs you find to do will have to become more involved as you go on, but in the meantime progress is being made. If you can share getting a job done with your horse, and take the lead while you're doing it, things can really move along for you both.

## The gypsy horseman

When you stick your head up above the parapet and get a bit of a name for doing this and that with horses, then everybody around wants to know what you are up to and how you are doing it. Nowadays, I don't say that I can necessarily solve any specific problem, but I do often say I'll give things a try and see if I might be able to make some difference.

A good friend of mine turned up at the yard accompanied by a gentleman I had not met before. He turned out to be a gypsy horseman and we had a bit of a yarn about this horse and that horse, and then he turned to me and said, 'All this natural horse stuff's nothing really is it? All they need is a load of work.' As hard as I try to keep a balanced head, that one threw me a bit, because I do put myself forward as offering something a bit different and it certainly isn't 'a load of work'. However, one thing I have realized is that if you take a horse and 'work' him, then after a time, if you're fair and consistent in your responses, that horse will nearly always reach a point where he accepts what you are doing and just gets on with it.

I often remember those few words of wisdom from that traveller. He owns a pair of driving horses and I have heard from two separate sources that they are perfect to drive right through the city centre of Birmingham. Everything he does with his horses he does very nicely; it's all very quietly done and the horses are more than happy with their lot.

I know that I want more than just acceptance from my horse, but sometimes it is a good place to start. If things are difficult and the horse is struggling to find some kind of order in what is going on, then a steady job can buy me the time to move things along. It is important to take the horse beyond his instinctive fears and anxieties. I need the horse to be with me, conscious of what I am asking of him, and making a conscious effort to carry out those requests. Depending on the situation, I can usually find some common ground where we can work together to develop our relationship to the point of good, straightforward communication. It may be something as simple as picking up feet, or it may be leading work, or something more demanding such as long lining in the pen or in the sand school.

● Whatever I do with my horse, I will be careful not to use work just to achieve some kind of surrender from him. I am looking for an understanding between us, but not the understanding between a hard master and a frightened servant. I want a relationship between willing partners where we each do our job to the best of our abilities because we both want to. To achieve this, I need to be sensitive to the state of the horse. I need to be sure that I give back to him something that he wants, in return for his giving me something that I want. If I can achieve this, then work is not a problem for either of us.

So why did I reel a bit when I first heard the traveller's wise words? Well, for a couple of reasons. First, because I know it's just not that easy: there are horses out there who need anything *but* 'work' to get them back on track; and second, because I know there are people out there using work to grind their horses down, and sometimes in the most awful of circumstances.

Look at this email from a client of mine, who owned a rather overweight pony that had just bucked off her young daughter.

'I asked Jo's instructor, who had originally fitted the saddle, to come over. She said Crabapple had become too fat, which caused it not to fit anymore. She advised half an hour of lunging twice a day to get the buck out of her, a 24-hour starvation paddock and a small amount of poor hay twice a day. Also, in relation to the bucking, she said that Jo should have hit her, got back on and gone round again!'

OK, so the pony *was* seriously overweight and something needed to be done to sort that out, and I know that the lunging and hitting advice was quite mild compared to a lot of what goes on, but it is a good example of the mentality a lot of people have when it comes to sorting out horse problems.

I like to approach these sorts of issues from exactly the opposite direction if I can. How about trying to look at things from the pony's point of view, and maybe let's try to give her some good reasons for getting it right that she can happily go along with? Does anyone out there seriously think it is a good idea to hit a pony that bucks because the saddle is hurting her? Of course not, but to one degree or another it goes on all the time.

When the traveller said, 'All they need is work,' he was assuming we would be getting an awful lot of other stuff right at the same time.

## Accept you're only human

Situations often arise where we humans are trying to find a way through our difficulties and almost can't help piling on more pressure. A good example is shouting at foreigners to get them to understand what we are saying – it just doesn't help at all. It is a natural instinct and it just happens. Sometimes when applied to horses it works, too, which reinforces the habit to a point where it just becomes a matter of course. What it amounts to is: if the horse doesn't understand what you want, then ask harder until he does. When it's put this way, most of us can soon work out the dangers of such a course of action, but it is not the way we always see it. Our human view is so often more a case of, 'Well, he knows what I want, he just doesn't want to do it.' And that is where the overwhelming desire to increase the pressure comes from.

We are used to dealing with humans in situations where we have clearly explained what we want and when our adversary shows any reluctance, we just raise the stakes a little by exhibiting some anger; then, if necessary, we just keep turning up the pressure until we get what we want. For the more powerful person involved in such a dispute it works a treat – they get what they want and they feel the 'power'; for the underdog, they quickly learn that an instant response can avoid a lot of unpleasantness. Next time things will run very smoothly.

A lot of people talk a lot about different ways of training animals, and a lot of people talk a lot about how best to train humans. With humans it's not usually called training: it's wrapped up in terms like goals and aims, careers, education, lifestyle and religion, but essentially it is training. I'm not saying humans are animals, and I'm not saying humans are not animals – I'm just saying that there are some huge similarities in the way we behave with each other and the way we behave with animals.

> ● **I think sometimes we make a big mistake at this point, because it is all too easy to think in human terms on behalf of the horse. When a horse hesitates for a few seconds**

before doing something he has been asked to do, it is often because he is not clear about what is being asked of him. In this instance, this is a totally inappropriate time to ask harder for what we want – doing that has the effect of increasing the anxiety in the horse, which more often than not just adds to the difficulty of the job. I always try to start from the point of view that I must be sure I am explaining to the horse exactly what it is that I want him to do. If he doesn't do it, then either I have not explained it well enough, or he does not trust me enough to do what I am asking. Neither of these two options is helped by piling on the pressure.

However, as I have said, we are human and that is what we do: we ask harder. I definitely do, I know I do, and I tell people who I'm working with to do it too. But if I find myself asking harder, what I also try to do is work harder to help the horse find the answer. A really simple example of this would be if I'm halter training a wild pony. I would ask him to move forward by putting a little pressure on the lead rope, and if he doesn't move forward I may up the pressure a tad, and then if he still doesn't get it I may move to the side to help him move his feet by pulling him slightly off balance. At the point at which he moves, he will feel the release of pressure and it won't take more than a couple of times for him to cotton on to the idea that the answer is to give to the pressure.

It is better by far to help out and get things moving than to become involved in a pitched battle of strength that ends in an all-out tug of war. If you try to make it easy for the horse then this seems to carry through to all that you do – it helps to bring the horse on to your side. It is as if he knows that you are trying to help him – you are with him, not against him.

# It all comes down to you

You can know and understand all the techniques and methods in the world, but in the end it all comes down to you making that one decision in each and every moment you are with your horse. So, how do you know when to do what?

When I am explaining to someone how I think things should be between them and their horse, I try very hard to keep everything as simple as possible. It has taken me 15 years to get from knowing nothing about horses to the point where now I go out and give people advice about situations they have got into with their horses. That is 15 years of knowledge and experience that I have worked hard to put together. I am quite an obsessive character and when I get into something I *really* get into it, so for long periods over those 15 years I have been totally and utterly involved in what I am doing. On top of this, I have specialized in quite a precise area of horsemanship, the area that is most relevant to me achieving my own personal goal with horses – to communicate with them to such an extent that I can establish a good working relationship with most horses quite quickly.

When I am first working with a client, I usually have about two hours to explain what I am up to and to show them how to do it as well. Fifteen years and two hours are quite a way apart (of course, I know that my client is not coming from nowhere in their experience, but to be honest, that can work both ways too). So the job is on for me: when I leave that yard, the client must have enough information and confidence to carry on the work that, hopefully, will lead them and their horse into a better relationship that will benefit them both. Sometimes, where horse and human are miles apart, this can be quite an extreme aim; at other times, it can be just a matter of adding one or two pointers to help someone who is already well on the way.

• • •

The ringing phone is where most jobs begin. A lot of my work seems to involve young horses that are pushing their owners around, and this particular job was another one of these. I had listened to the lady on the phone for quite a long time, more than once thinking how lucky that the call was on her bill and not mine. From that call, I kind of knew it was going to be quite difficult for me to get through to her, mainly because she already knew so much about horses. I tried a couple of times to indicate that maybe we could work on some things that might help the relationship get back on track, but to no avail. I learnt about the horse's breeding, and her history, and her character, her price, and what lay ahead for her in the future. I learnt where the horse lived and who the lady knew and who she had worked with before and, perhaps most important of all, I learnt how much her house was worth and that she wasn't planning on selling it anyway.

So, armed with all this information, I arrived at the house and met this very sweet lady who already had the kettle on and the cups set for coffee. That's my kind of client, I thought, as my eyes spotted the cake tin also at the ready. I remembered back to my days in the building industry when we had a cast-iron policy of never, ever, saying no to a cup of tea, even if you'd just had one the second before you knocked on the door – the theory being that if you say no once, you may never get asked again. Then you are faced with what is known as the 'dry job syndrome', where the day is taken up with interminable hints to the client about the dusty atmosphere and unseasonably hot weather.

Another thing I noticed about this lady was that she was very small and also quite elderly. I knew from the phone call that the horse was a three-year-old 15.2hh thoroughbred and I knew that she had been riding it around too. I was expecting the worst. We went outside to the paddock and there she was, an absolutely gorgeous filly, and I immediately made my standard offer of £500 for her. No, of course I didn't, but she was pretty and I was tempted, especially as the client kept on talking about how she might not be able to cope. By this time, I had also learnt that quite often when being ridden, the horse had taken over completely, spun around and run off home. I was seriously worried for this little old lady's future, not to mention what chaos she might cause to anyone else.

I went up to the horse, put on the halter and started doing my usual stuff: just a little ask back and a little walk and a halt and so on. The horse had no idea at all. She was walking through me, she couldn't concentrate for more than a second on anything, and she walked off whenever she felt like it. Even with my strength, it was all I could do to hold her. God only knows how the owner managed. How on earth did she get her tacked up, climb into the saddle and go for a ride? The whole situation was verging on madness in my view.

Now, sometimes it is surprising how quickly things can be turned around just by offering a bit of clarity, but with this one I couldn't get through at all. We were working in a small orchard that was full of really long grass and it was quite a struggle to walk through it, plus the horse was so scatty she hardly noticed I was there. You know the saying, 'Don't set yourself up for a loser'? Well, that's where I was right then, but I'd travelled a long way to the job and although I could see the jam I was in I really had no choice, so I carried on. After what seemed a very long time, but was actually only about 45 minutes, I had the horse leading around in some fashion but not anything like I would want it before I would go any further. And then it came, the bolt from the blue: 'Can you load her into the lorry? I need to take her to the school because it is too far to ride. I can get her in, but she keeps rushing out before I can get the ramp up.'

You know, there is this modern phrase 'reality check'. How far away from reality was this lady, and what hope was there of me ever getting anything across to her that would help her move this job along? I really needed to be out of that place, but there was no way I could leave things as they were. She was a very sweet lady who had had horses all her life and was somehow completely oblivious to the size of the tasks she was undertaking here. I can't believe it happened, but I ended up loading that horse into the lorry, then teaching her to stand still while we shut the ramp and to stand still again while we opened it back up. On top of all this, the little old lady loaded the horse too. I swear to God she did not listen to a word I said that day, and I left knowing she didn't have a hope in hell of doing what she wanted to do. But she was as optimistic as ever. I told her to practise loading in a safe place for a few days before going out into the big wide world, thinking that then she would realize the whole thing was a non-starter. The next day I got a call from her: she'd got to the school no problem, but she couldn't load the horse for the return journey. She had decided the horse was too much for her and she was swapping her for an old Highland pony. Hooray!

So, did I learn anything from my day out at that job? I sure did, and I've learnt it a lot of times since – it's not about getting horses to do things, it's about getting across to people how to be with horses, and that doesn't always happen in two hours. It's a big commitment for people to make and it isn't always high on the list of goals they want to achieve with their horses. But if it is their goal, then it is a very achievable one.

# In the moment

Many times I have watched someone working with a horse and felt that if only they had done this instead of that, things would have gone better. Then again, many times people have done something that has turned out better than I thought it would. Making decisions in each moment is a very personal thing.

The other day I was out in the field with the horses and I needed to put a rug on one of them. He was a big working horse that belonged to a friend of mine and was used for pulling logs. Since he had been with us I had hardly had anything to do with him. As I went to put the halter on him, he just walked off and wouldn't let me catch him. I admit I was in a bit of a hurry and my initial thoughts were roughly along the lines of, 'No way, I don't need this sort of thing right now.' As soon as I saw him begin to walk I just upped the pressure on him without even thinking about it – I walked after him with all my energy directed right at him. He was a bit surprised and took off a little bit faster, and I turned it up a bit more. I wasn't expecting him to walk off in the first place and my reactions happened so fast that I did it all in the moment without giving it a second thought.

By now I was realizing that I might have made an horrendous mistake, and I began to imagine the next hour or so of messing about in all the mud with this horse giving me the complete runaround. Thanks be, the horse-catching gods were with me: within five seconds he had decided he didn't need the pressure and he stopped in his tracks. I went soft immediately and he knew he'd got it right – and the job was done.

Of course, it could all have gone horribly wrong. What could have been one rash decision by me in that moment might have led to a very different sequence of events. In earlier years I spent many frustrating hours trying to catch horses that had other ideas, and it was no fun. I have thought a lot about those few seconds with the big horse over the last day or two, because for me what happened there is, in a nutshell, what working with horses is all about: being here now, making a decision, acting on it and dealing with the consequences.

The ability to make the right decisions only comes from practice and experience. No-one always gets it right either, but what we can do is play the percentages and make the decisions that, if they do go wrong, have the least disastrous consequences. Doing what I did there with that heavy horse in a 12-acre field, for example, had a potentially much more serious downside than if I'd done it in a 50ft-diameter round pen. Over and over you can see the value of setting things up for success. Admittedly, you can never completely rule out the possibility of getting it wrong – that's part of the game – but if you are going to get serious about this stuff you need to start looking at all the ways in which you can help to lessen the gamble in the work that you do.

## Making judgements

I try to be in a space within myself where I am free from pressure, and free from stress. If I am relaxed, soft and (excuse the expression) 'in the flow', then working out what to do isn't really an issue. How does it happen? I don't know, but it just does. I used to watch trainers very carefully to try to work out what they were doing. I guess I was looking for their systems and for little pointers that would show me how to get results with my horses. But now when I watch trainers I am looking to see how they *are* with the horse far more than what they are *doing* with the horse.

Many people have marketed methods and systems of things to do with your horse, and for sure you can get results by following these. You can work your way down the list and then move on to the next list, and then move up to the next level, and so on and so on. But in the end, the main thing you will learn is that no matter what technique you use, if you are not in the right place within yourself, then the results will not be as good as if you were. Your horse knows if you are there with him, or not.

I love to walk up to my horse feeling good and let him feel that I am just fine to be with. Horses are so sensitive to feelings and often you can get half the job done before you even begin. Of course, there are some practical things that can be done to help set things up in a good way for both of us, too. It is good to move around horses in a non-threatening way, without too many sudden movements and without making huge unexpected amounts of noise. Take care to notice that your horse is comfortable with where you are and what you are doing. If you are causing him anxiety, then back off a bit to a point that he is happy with and work from there. This is a crucial point, which is at the heart of the decisions you need to take about what to do with your horse and when to do it: every time you ask your horse to do something he is not comfortable with, in his mind he marks you down as a problem. If you can ask him several times in a row to do things with which he has no problem, then hopefully he will mark you down as no problem too. After that, you stand a good chance of making progress into those areas that previously were totally no go.

Several years ago I sold a young colt to a very experienced horsewoman who runs a yard some miles away from ours. Jay is good at the work she does and takes in a lot of difficult horses herself. One thing I particularly like about the way she works is the patience she has with the horses. She thinks nothing of giving a horse weeks and months to come to terms with his problems and worries, if she thinks that is what he needs. There was one mare in her yard that had come badly unstuck very early on in her ridden career when the saddle had slipped under her belly. It was several months before that horse was happy to have the girth tightened and a rider up on her back again, but Jay got the job done and that horse eventually went out into the world completely fine with the whole idea.

A couple of years after Jay bought my colt, she called me up about an unhandled five-year-old cob that she had bought off the moor.

She had had the horse for about eight weeks and she still hadn't managed to get a headcollar on him. In her usual patient way, she was prepared to take as long as it takes, but she was a bit concerned that things had apparently got completely stuck.

I went down to the yard and Jay told me that she could touch the horse on the shoulder, but as soon as she tried to move on from there the horse wheeled away and turned his back end on her. I quietly went into the stable and slowly approached the horse. As soon as had I managed to touch his shoulder gently, I drew back a couple of steps and stood quietly for a few seconds. My plan here was to show the horse that being touched by me was not a problem. I repeated this a couple of times, each time taking into account how well the horse was coping with my advances. As I could see that he was fine with what I was doing, I gradually enlarged the area of contact for a few seconds before retreating again. Within two or three minutes I could see that the horse was beginning to feel very relaxed with my approach, so I started working in the same way but this time with the halter in my hand.

The job continued really smoothly, and before the end of the session we were leading the horse around the yard with no trouble. Jay was able to go into the stable and put on the halter, and from there I knew she would have no problems.

So, what is the point of this story and what was I doing so differently to Jay that could make such a huge difference to the results we each achieved? First, the most important thing in a job like this – and, indeed, in any job – is to gauge whatever you are doing by the way that the horse reacts. For me, two-way communication is everything as far as working with horses is concerned. Second – and the amount of difference this made to this job surprised me as much as it did Jay – just putting in those retreats allowed me to gain the horse's trust within minutes. Without them Jay had not managed to get this trust in weeks of good work. It was a huge

*'My plan here was to show the horse that being touched by me was not a problem. I repeated this a couple of times, each time taking into account how well the horse was coping with my advances.'*

lesson for us both. As we drove away, I joked to Sarah that the last person I should have shown that to was Jay, as there would be no stopping her now and I doubted our phone would ever ring again.

Jay is a good horsewoman and soon after our visit she was back in touch to let us know how well things were going with the cob. Good luck to her, and long may she continue to help out troubled horses.

# All in all

Before moving on to the next chapter, I just want to run through some of the ideas I have discussed so far and really focus on what I think are the important points to establish in your relationship with your horse.

First and foremost is your state of mind. You need to be calm and rational, and your actions need to be logical and consistent. These qualities are really important to horses and can make a huge difference in the way that they respond to you. I have seen horses change their view of someone simply by that person walking in a more positive way. If you want to be your horse's leader, then you have to offer him someone whom he considers worth following, whom he perceives as knowing where they are going, and whom he sees as both trustworthy and reliable.

When your horse takes on this kind of belief, then he will let you get things done – until then, it will most likely be a bit of a struggle. Of course, you need to realize that to get to a point where the horse allows you into his life with no questions asked is obviously much easier with some horses than with others. There are many factors, such as the horse's breeding, his history and even what you are trying to do with him, that will determine the results that you get. If the task is to touch your horse on the shoulder and your horse is a good solid cob that has never been off the farm, your job is obviously going to be less of a challenge than, say, applying medicinal cream to a sore place high up between the back legs of a highly bred and badly abused Arabian horse.

● But one thing is for sure: whatever the job, the approach is always the same. You need to show the horse that you are not a threat and that he can trust you. Remember, the horse's number one instinct is survival and if you are not a threat to him on this front then you can begin to do business. If you are always aware of this one simple fact then the perspective with which you approach the job won't be far wrong. At the same time, don't make the mistake of thinking that approaching in a totally non-threatening way is all the horse needs. Your horse is looking for safety and that doesn't come from a wishy-washy and unconvincing attitude. Your horse is looking for sureness and strength, something he can really rely on for his well-being. Horses are very sensitive and perceptive beings – they can feel safety.

Next, remember the two important things that all horses need to know – and if you watch almost all successful trainers you will see that they are doing both these things, whether they know it or not. Make your personal space very clear, and control the movement of your horse. These two things are foremost in the horse's mind and if you don't get down to business on these jobs fairly swiftly you will almost certainly be giving some very mixed messages to your horse. Sometimes we get into situations with our horses where it begins to feel a bit like the whole job is just too big and way beyond our capabilities. I would never come out and say that is not the case because it might well be, but don't underestimate the worth of a little bit of correct knowledge. I remember one evening

I unexpectedly ended up holding a big unruly mare while a couple of friends of mine set up the lorry to try and load her. I was feeling good that night and I backed her quietly and gently out of my space and stood still with her for just a few minutes. I couldn't really have done much less with this horse but by the time the guys got back to me the change was so great in the horse they jokingly accused me of drugging her.

Now of course it's not always like this by any means, but one thing is for sure, the principles never change. Get things right, stand your ground, and over time the job will surely start to go your way.

# Being Alive

· · · · · · · · · · · · ·

When I was a child, I really wanted to feel Christmas so about 15 minutes to midnight on Christmas Eve I went up to the church and stood outside the door and listened to the people inside singing carols. I'd been there a few minutes when this old guy came up to meet his wife as she came out of the church. He asked me why I was standing outside and not inside with all the other people. So I asked him why he wasn't in there too. He told me straight out that he didn't believe in God but his wife did, and then he asked me if I believed in God.

Now, I was just a kid who didn't know much about anything, so it was a bit of a big question for me. I'd been to church loads of times, because we were Catholics and we used to go to church every Sunday. I'd done confessions and had Holy Communion, but to be honest I never quite believed what the priest was saying.

Anyway, I didn't answer the old man's question about God and a few seconds later he asked me if I believed in ghosts. I hadn't got a clue about this one either. I knew I was scared of them, but whether they were real or not, I had no idea. I was stalling on answering this too when the carol singing stopped, the doors opened and the people started streaming out into the cold night. I watched them all go by and thought about their nice warm houses full of Christmassy stuff, and how sure about everything they all looked, and wondered if I was the only person in the world who didn't quite realize what was going on.

I still get that feeling sometimes, when I see people who are somehow so certain about their lives. Sometimes I go into people's houses and everything is in place, there are really nice scented leaves and flowers in the hall and beautiful curtains at all the windows.

And I'm thinking, 'Have I missed something here?'

But now I know one thing that is very helpful to me, one thing that is the same for every human being on this planet earth, and that is: all that really exists for each of us is now. When I walked back from that church and into my house, and saw the decorations and the tree, that feeling of Christmas was real to me then.

If you put yourself into that moment called now, what is there? Does anything else exist except you, here, now? Are you okay with that? I'll tell you what, you can get to like it, because when you are there you are free.

So what is the point of this Christmas story, and what relevance has it to horses? Simply, that the very best way to be with your horse is to be here now. Horses can relate to that because it is what they do themselves. They don't have plans, or ambitions, or agendas. They are just there, feeling their lives and getting on with them. Of all the creatures on this planet, it is probably only we humans who lose the moment to our thoughts.

# Your side of the deal

*I remember the first course I went on to learn about horses. I knew a bit already – after all, I'd spent a few years looking after my stallion and his herd – but because I had no upbringing in so-called conventional horsemanship I really knew very little about things like tacking up and all the little rights and wrongs that seem to go on in the horse world. I was worried that I might try to get on the horse from the wrong side (I still do that sometimes), or maybe forget the order in which the tack has to be put on (I still do that too).*

It was a really good course that was run by Kelly Marks and her organization, Intelligent Horsemanship. I had a tough time that week. For one thing, it was all girls except for me and a guy from Ireland called Donal. He was an experienced horseman and, thankfully, we got on well. When I look back, I realize I was absolutely petrified of making a fool of myself, and I guess that wasn't made any easier by all the female company. My male ego was feeling very vulnerable that week.

On a practical level, one thing I really struggled with early on in the week was projecting my energy towards the horse in such a way that he would move away from me. It was something I had never, ever attempted to do before, and it was pretty much the opposite to what I had been trying to do with my horses, and in nearly every other part of my life, up to that point. I had never really looked at the possibility of moving anything away from me. If I didn't want something near me, I just moved away from it. And that just about sums up how I was at that time: I was 'Mr Accommodating' on a grand scale and, as I've since realized, that is one thing horses don't find so easy to deal with.

On the second day of the course I was rather taken aback, as first thing in the morning I was pulled out of the group for some special lessons in projecting my energy. This was a difficult task for me because, as I've explained, my energy was well and truly buried, and had been for years. I did finally manage to find that power within me, but it wasn't easy. There I was, standing facing another student about a metre away, and then we were told to get the other person to move back without using any physical force. Nowadays I reckon I could move just about anybody, but back then could I get her to move? No way – I didn't know where to start. So up stepped the teacher and showed us what to do. There was so much power coming out of that girl, fierce eye contact and lots of forward movement into my space. I promise you that moving back was the only option.

● Those few minutes out there away from the rest of the group were a turning point for me in my life with horses. Seeing that power and beginning to feel it within me began to open up all sorts of possibilities. It also allowed me to begin to understand how horses communicate with each other. All my ideas about horse language, which presumably I had formed based on my ideas about human communication, began to dissolve and I began to see a language not of words, concepts or ideas, but of energy. It is a language so easy to learn and yet so fascinating that I have been studying it ever since. I like it, and it suits me because it is not a language that requires super-intelligence or great learning ability, but it is a language that can be practised, and the more you practise it the better you can get at it, and the better you get at it the more

**powerful and useful it becomes. From the humble beginnings of asking for a simple move away from you to the really good stuff like getting a wild horse to accept your touch – it's all the same language.**

# Learn from where you are

So, in the same way that you would learn any task, you need to start off your communication with horses simply and at a level where you can get a result, and build on that. I have never managed to learn to play a musical instrument, but I know the process is the same. The first two or three times you try to play a chord it requires a real conscious effort, but each subsequent time it just becomes easier (although this was absolutely not my experience with a guitar – it never got any easier for me, ever!), until you actually begin to do it without any effort at all. That's how it will become between you and your horse, but it may take a little time. If a horse moves into my space now, I don't think about it: I just move him back. I never stop working my horses, but it's not like work, to them or to me, it's just how we are, automatically and constantly aware of each other.

I once worked as a driving instructor and one day I had to teach an elderly lady. I turned up at her house first thing in the morning as arranged. She was extremely pleasant and we got on very well. After going through a few of the basics, I decided that she might as well give it a go. I had dual controls so I was never scared in situations like that – it just felt as if I was driving the car but from the other side. However, that day I was in for a surprise. This lady couldn't steer – something I had never come across before. What is almost a natural act for most people, she just couldn't do. We were all over the place, because she couldn't judge the connection between the turn in the steering wheel and the turn in the wheels. And then, when the car did turn one way she would drastically over-compensate the other way, so we had a right old time of it. We were literally all over the road.

It took four lessons for that lady to get to point where we could travel along the road in first gear with her completely in control of the direction of the car. She didn't care: she just assumed that learning to steer was part of learning to drive anyway. For me it was a bit of a shock, because I was used to 'learning to steer' being something that happened automatically.

So, at first it was very hard work for my student, but as she practised it became easier. It's so obvious, isn't it? In the end she was steering without thinking about it – it had become totally natural for her. At that point we were able to move on to more challenging things, like changing gear and clutch control. Can you imagine how much fun that was?

Before moving on from my time as a driving instructor, I have to mention just one other client of mine. Eileen started off as a student of my boss, Rick. After something like 150 lessons and failing her test six times, he asked me if I would take over for a while to give him a break. No worries, it's all the same to me I thought, as I took on the challenge like the man I was. I worked really hard with Eileen, but after another 30 lessons and a couple more failed tests, I threw in the towel. My days as a driving instructor were over – not because of Eileen, I'd just had enough of sitting in a car all day long.

I saw Rick a year or two later and the first question I asked him was, 'How did things go with Eileen?' All credit to Rick for sticking with it, and to Eileen for the same reason. She had passed her test at the ninth attempt and was now free to drive wherever and whenever she wanted to, a remarkable achievement for someone whom we had both more or less written off as a bit of a joke. Maybe if I had shown the same kind of dedication to playing the guitar that Eileen showed towards learning to drive, I would now be a famous rock star.

# Fantasy versus reality

One thing I have noticed about the world of horses is that, almost without exception, the people involved in it spend most of their time dreaming of what could be, rather than what actually is. I know I do. When I get rich and have a bit more time on my hands, the first thing I'm going to do is buy my dream horse. I know exactly what she's like, I rode her once and for some reason I'll never understand, I didn't try to buy her. She was a ten-year-old thoroughbred mare, quite small, about 15.1hh, not particularly well built – some would say she was a bit scraggy – but boy was she comfortable. And what a joy she was: she just seemed to know where I wanted to go; it was the best experience.

It was years ago that I rode that horse, but my dream lives on. And I still believe I will find her, I've no idea where. I will be riding across the moor on my beautiful horse, and of course she loves me as much as I love her. We are unbelievable together. If we need to go somewhere we just go there, if we need a break we just take one. If jets fly overhead we don't care, if tractors come roaring towards us we just deal with it, no problem. And then when my mare is about 15 she breeds the most incredible foal you have ever seen, and the dream begins again, only this time it's even better.

It's almost more fun dreaming my dreams than it is getting on with what is really going on. That thing called reality – what your horse is really like, the situation you are really in – that is where you have to begin. I'm not giving up my dreams, but at the same time I do have to get real about what is happening right now.

• • •

Lorna called me up and told me all about her horses. She had bought three of them from a lady down the road. There was a four-year-old untouched mare, as wild as they come, with her six-month-old foal and another weaned foal to keep him company, both as wild as the mare, too. Pretty scary stuff really, but even more scary was that, when I went to see them, I had only been there for about five minutes and Lorna had already told me exactly what she had planned out for each horse over the next few years. One of the foals was going to be her daughter's riding horse and the other was for her. The mare, which, according to Lorna, might be a bit more work, was going to do a bit of competing and maybe later on breed another foal.

Great plans. So let's make a start then, shall we? Let's see if we can find a way of getting near any of these horses without getting our heads kicked in.

I know I'm being a bit cynical here, but I see this going on over and over. It doesn't matter at all – as long as you realize that, regardless of the dreams, you still have to do the job: you have to put in the leg work. I guess what I am saying here is that it is important that you start from somewhere near to reality. (By the way, I'm talking reality in the worldly sense here – knowing the 'real' reality would probably be an asset too, but I'm pretty sure it's not an essential for this kind of work.)

In most circumstances, when you are working with your horse, if you see a job that needs doing it is nearly always a good idea to get on and do it. For example, if you dream of doing dressage on your horse, no-one need ever know that he won't stand still for you to get on – they won't see you mounting, will they? So you may be tempted to spend your time working on the more important stuff that might gain you a few extra marks in the test, rather than fiddling about working on the mounting, which scores you nothing. But, look at it like this – your horse can't even stand still for you to get on him, so everything else that you put on top of that is built on a faulty foundation. Leaving 'holes' in your horse's training is asking for trouble later on. Getting it right from the foundations up is the correct way to do the job.

Similarly, it is important not to leave holes in your own training. A while ago I was talking to a young girl who just loved competing; in fact, she described her perfect day as attending a one-day event. I have no doubt that she was a good rider: that very day while out hunting she had jumped a five-bar gate on her magnificent horse when rushing to attend to someone who had had an unfortunate accident nearby.

I was talking to this girl that day because there were some loading issues with her horse that needed looking at. When we got home that evening and unloaded the horses, I could see why. That brilliant rider was really not so good when she was on the ground: the horse was walking through her and she didn't even realize it was happening. He butted into her head and she just let it go as if she hadn't even noticed. I called out to her not to let that happen. She looked around, wondering what I was talking about. She had no conception that the reason her horse was struggling with things like leading and loading was because she was completely overlooking the importance of her relationship with him. For her, the horse achieved everything that she wanted, and the fact that the loading was poor was, in her words, 'because he's got a screw loose'. The truth was that the horse didn't have a screw loose at all: he just needed better attention, and her groundwork was full of holes.

# Give yourself time

I got to a point with my horse work where I decided that I would advertise my services to help other people with their horse problems. It was not a step I took lightly. I wanted the experience of working with lots of different horses with lots of different issues, and for my own interest and improvement I needed continually to face the challenge of communicating with the horse. But those first few months were no picnic for me. It was a minefield of uncertainty while I learnt how to deal with individual clients and the various issues they were trying to sort out with their horses. I also had to learn to deal with failure, which was probably the most difficult thing of all for me.

One of the lessons I learnt quickest from 'failure' was that, in the end, some jobs just need time. Nowadays, I might even change that statement to 'all jobs just need time' – for goodness' sake, what is the hurry anyway? Well, I guess that the hurry on a lot of jobs is caused by economic pressure, and there's not a lot anyone can do about that. I was watching a demonstration once and someone in the audience asked the trainer, 'Have you ever failed?' The guy gave a great answer. Quick as a flash, he said, 'No, but I have run out of time.' What I try to do now is make sure that I leave the client with a plan of action and a measure of ability to try to take the job forward themselves.

The very first day I was officially called out as a professional horse trainer will stay in my memory for a long time. I had two horses to visit within about ten miles of each other, and I had set it up to do one in the morning and the other in the afternoon. I knew that it was important that I got off to a flyer. I was very aware that a knockback at this point would have been quite tough for me to recover from.

I pulled into the first yard. At this time I had a questionnaire that I asked the client to fill in before I started work. I don't do this any more, because I feel that it just takes up 20 minutes finding out things about the horse, most of which I don't need to know, and most of which the owner tells me as we go along anyway. Looking back, one good thing about that questionnaire was that on most jobs I would get invited in for a cup of tea while we worked our way through it. Also, I think a lot of people just like talking through lots of stuff about their horse. It reminds me of the first time I went to see an alternative medical practitioner. He spent the first half hour asking me all sorts of searching questions about myself: it felt really good just having someone take so much notice of me. I was used to the five-minute consultation and obligatory prescription for some antibiotics that is the way of our beloved health service. Which way works best? I'll keep my options open on that one.

The first horse I visited that day was just like so many other horses I have worked with since. He was pushy and bitey and basically pretty grouchy. The owner was becoming a little bit scared of him and things were going from bad to worse. I would probably do things slightly differently now, but what I did worked well enough. I worked the horse on a lead rope in the sand school and used some poles and mazes to get him concentrating. The lead I was giving him was just about enough to stop him from biting me and before long we were doing some nice work. Before I left, I got the owner to go through all the exercises I had been practising and asked her to do some groundwork every day just to keep the relationship set up in a way she was happy with. Although I didn't know it at the time, what I was actually asking her to do was make the decisions about her horse's movement, speed and direction – all things that to the horse would indicate she was in charge.

Before I left, I did one more thing. For a while I wondered whether I should say anything, and then I screwed up my courage and blurted it out. The design of the stable yard could have been half the reason that the horse was in trouble. There were four stables in a row and the fifth was around the corner facing the other way. It was like an extreme L shape but with the horses on the outside instead of the normal inside. The troubled horse was totally isolated around the corner. Of course, I might have been wrong but to me it didn't look as if it was helping.

I never heard from that yard again, so I have no idea how things went on after I left. I tend to take silence as a sign that things didn't work out, but it's not necessarily the case. Often months afterwards I get another call saying that things have all changed around because of my visit, and can I come again to help with a friend's horse.

I stopped at a garage on my way to the next job and bought myself a sandwich and a drink. I felt good, because I knew I had got that horse on my side. However, I didn't feel so sure that the owner was convinced by my work, and to a degree I felt that I should have tried harder to get across to her that what I was proposing would be helpful to both her and her horse.

I pulled into the next yard about an hour later to see a horse called Shy. I got out of the car with my clipboard and sure enough was invited in for another cup of tea. As I went through my questionnaire, I began to get a little bit worried, mainly because the owner, Jenny, kept saying things like, 'And then, for no reason, he just rears up.' A big part of me really likes to have a reason why things are happening. Then I feel that if I can take away that reason perhaps those things won't happen. But if things truly are happening for no reason, where on earth do you start?

Anyway, I was a professional horse trainer so there was no way I could show my doubts and confusion; I just had to get out there and crack on with the job. I was expecting the worst as I approached the stable. I went in and put the halter on Shy, expecting to be attacked at any time for 'absolutely no reason'. Thankfully, good luck was with me that day, or maybe it was because of something I was doing inadvertently. Shy was fine. He just got on with what I asked of him, and by the end of the session I was pretty much able to do everything that Jenny had been struggling with over the previous few weeks. To be honest, at the time I had no idea why Shy had been so good for me. But now I know what I did: I asked Shy to do a few things, and when he did them I rewarded him – not with titbits, but with 'nothing'. He could relate to this; he took me on board as someone he could work with and away we went.

If you are reading this and thinking, 'How many more times is he going to tell us about situations that he goes into and yet again, without telling us what he's done, it all ends up fine' – well, I'm kind of doing that on purpose, because what I'm trying to show each time is that it's not what you *do*, it's the way that you *are*. For the record, with Shy I walked him over a few poles and took him through a couple of mazes, but really it could have been anything. All Shy needed to know was that I am a reliable, consistent, logical, fair and generous being with whom he felt secure and from whom he could take a lead. It wasn't the poles, or the lead rope – it was what I was offering him from within me. Shy was looking at me to see if what I was offering was good enough for him. He based his decision on what he saw and felt.

## Hang on in there

I drove home that day feeling good. I knew I could get (at least some) troubled horses on my side, which was all I wanted to know. As I said, I never heard again from my first client, but a year later Jenny wrote me a letter. She had carried on the exercises with Shy and he had been great for months afterwards, but recently things had started to go a bit off-course again. A few days later Shy came up to our yard to stay for a couple of weeks.

'Someone's got to do the worrying.' That's what a friend of mine used to say in all seriousness, as though every task that had to be accomplished carried with it some requisite amount of anxiety with which we had to cope. I don't really buy into that theory, I know that worry comes from the mind and is not necessarily based on logic and reality. But all that said, I have to admit I was just born the kind of guy that worries; if I've got a job to do, I go over it again and again in my mind trying to sort out all the 'how tos' and 'what ifs' of the whole thing. I know it would be better if I could just focus on the 'now', as I'm sure all my fellow worriers do too. This morning I heard a smug pundit on the radio saying that worrying is pointless. His actual words were, 'Why worry about something you can do nothing about?' For me, it's not that simple – I just do worry. I try to keep it in some kind of perspective, but boy, it's hard not to let it affect how I am.

When I heard that Shy was up to all his old 'nonsense' again, I started to worry about what I was going to say and do to help get him and Jenny through their current crisis. To Jenny, Shy's behaviour was all such a mystery and, like the last time, it was all happening for no reason, so yet again we went into the job without much idea of what to do. But by now I was beginning to cotton on to a bit of a theme in the work I was doing – there really weren't lots of different problems, but there were lots of different symptoms all of the same problem. So this time I just knew that things would more than likely go well if we could get the feel right between us and the horse.

Jenny and I worked hard for two weeks filling in all the holes in Shy's relationship with humans and sure enough he did come good, but the point of the story is that four years later Jenny and Shy are still working together and things are going from good to better to best. Shy is a very happy horse in pretty much every area of his life, and to me he is an inspirational example of what can be achieved through patience, understanding and dedication. It has to be more than just theory for me. I don't want to be making a living out of hot air. I know it all sounds great to go on about gentle this and kindness that, but people need to see it working. We need to see the horses responding to the way we are with them. In the wise words of Keith Richard, 'Talk is cheap'.

# Can you learn 'feel'?

'Feel' is a word that a lot of people use when it comes to working with horses. When I first heard it I couldn't quite get hold of what it meant, but after a while I started to experience something that I thought might be it. It was feeling as if I was with my horse and he was with me, and we were somehow working together in some kind of harmony. I first used to feel it in the lead rope and in my hand when I was leading the horse. I could talk to him through the lead rope. We've got this narrow little gate that we have to lead through to get to the big field, and when you're taking two horses at a time it can be a bit tricky getting them through it. Trying to negotiate this one day, I realized that the horse could feel the smallest little signal through the rope, and I could feel his response in my hands. It was like magic.

• • •

I have to be honest: I don't really enjoy some of the horse jobs I get asked to do. It's a kind of bitter-sweet thing, where I want to do the job because I want to learn, and I don't want to do the job because I know it will take me to the edge of my ability. I will probably feel scared and nervous, and I will be close to failure. There is this dreadful saying, 'You are only as good as your last job', and the awful thing is that that is how you feel. When it does work out you feel high as a kite, but when it doesn't you don't feel so good at all. And, the bigger the challenge, the more likely you are to draw the short straw.

When the phone rang and Faye asked me to help her with her bucking horse, Cruse, I really didn't want to know. I've been down that road and there are so many downsides, it's rarely worth the risk. I tried my best to get out of it, but underneath it all I couldn't

'We've got this narrow little gate that we have to lead through to
get to the big field. Negotiating this one day, I realized that the
horse could feel the smallest little signal through the rope, and
I could feel his response in my hands. It was like magic.'

escape the fact that there was a part of me that couldn't resist it. All credit to Faye, she didn't let up and after three weeks I said I would take a look at the horse. I'm going to tell the story about Cruse later, but I want to tell you part of it right now because it is all about 'feel'.

We eventually got to the point where I was happy to put my rider up on Cruse. She got on the horse and he settled down and I let him go. There was so much feel from that rider towards that horse that he just knew he had someone on his back who understood him. The communication going on between the two was awesome, and this was a horse that had been chucking people off for fun and for months. Now, can you learn that feel? Well, all I can say is that I have learnt something of it because there was definitely a time when I had no idea myself, and the horses knew that too. Now I know that horses feel my feel, and boy it feels good when that happens. I think back to the days with my first stallion, when he was all over me, and the little stallion man, without even knowing it, just used feel to transform him into a contented and happy animal.

● In some way feel is experience – but it's not just that, is it? Because there are people who have worked with horses for decades and are no further down the road with the way they do it now than when they first started. There has to be a desire and a need within you to find it. Maybe feel comes to you if you want it to. I know this is a personal view, nothing more, but from watching good horse trainers I really do believe that finding feel is connected to something within. It is in some way linked to some kind of humility, some kind of softness, some kind of surrender to a greater good. How many times have you heard people say that horses are great levellers? How many times have you experienced that very same thing?

I was working on a television programme with Tony, a youngster who had been in trouble with the law and who had something called 'anger management problems'. He was concerned that a lot of his problems came about just because of the way he came across: maybe he was giving off the feeling to people that he was never that far away from exploding into trouble and getting into fights, and because of this, other guys were having a pop at him to see if they could wind him up.

The producer of the documentary, Henrietta, had the idea that if Tony worked with me and the horses, he would be able to see the powerful effect that his presence was having on other beings in his immediate environment, and maybe by becoming more conscious of this, he could then do something about it. I'd got talked into this job when a researcher rang me up to get my views on whether working with horses might help troubled youngsters get their lives back on track.

The initial meeting between Tony and me was quite a dramatic moment. I feared he would be some big, violent guy and he feared I would be some overbearing, sergeant major-type – as it turned out we were both pleasantly surprised. Tony was quite a quiet, humble guy who thought things through and was beginning to see which direction he didn't want his life to go in. We got on really well.

Like a lot of kids in the western world today, Tony's prospects weren't really anywhere near the goals presented to him as acceptable or successful by the media and the powers that be – the reality and the fantasy were a very long way apart. Often, the major challenge for a lot of young people is coming to terms with their total inability to make an impact on the massive task in front of them. Getting a job, getting a car, getting a house and getting a family; for some kids, this all appears such an undoable task that they end up like rabbits caught in the headlights – they just freeze and await their fate.

Henrietta had a theme going through the documentary all about this body-language theory, so she needed to get me to say something along those lines. But I couldn't really say what she needed to hear, because I know that when it comes down to it, your body language is just a reflection of your inner state. If you feel a certain way, that's the way you will look. Which comes first, looking confident or feeling confident – it's obvious really, isn't it?

And that's how horses see it too, except that they are far sharper than the average human when it comes to sussing out how we are feeling. We could go in there with all the 'right' signals – you know, the submissive shoulders or the full eye contact, whatever you want – but if it's not backed up with the genuine feeling, it doesn't mean a lot to the horse.

When I look back to those couple of days' work that Tony and I did together, I can see that, to a degree, I did explain to him how it's best to move around horses in a quiet, smooth sort of a way, and it's best not to make too many big sudden movements, but what I mostly did was just work with him around the horses, and as his confidence grew so his body language reflected this. So, in terms of Tony's life back in the big city, did Henrietta want me to say that if only Tony could learn to enter a night club and keep his eyes soft and focused on the floor, have his shoulders slightly hunched and his fingers relaxed in a passive way, then people wouldn't see him as some kind of legitimate target for a wind-up? Some of that would almost certainly help, but I think the very best way to strike up a non-threatening pose is to have a non-threatening attitude.

● **When it comes to working with horses, you need to start from the premise that if it's real within you then it will come out. If your problem is, for example, that you are a little scared of picking up your horse's back feet, then don't just wade** in there putting on a brave face, trying to fool yourself as well as your horse. Instead, work inside the boundaries you are comfortable with and allow your confidence to build up naturally. That confidence from you will then come through to your horse and you may find that things proceed a good deal quicker than you originally thought they would.

# Find that softness

I eventually got the stallion to go into the lorry. It wasn't easy. He had been 'not going in the lorry' for several years, so it was a big change for him to make. I took him in and out a few times and then I said to the owner, 'Do you want to see if he'll go in with you?'

'No problem,' she replied briskly, grabbing hold of the lead rope. I could see that I needed to slow her down, so I stopped her right there and asked her if she could go and get herself a hard hat. I was beginning to wish I had spent more time explaining that a bit of softness around the place would help things go a long way in the right direction. Sometimes I hate this job, it's just too difficult!

In no time at all she was back and off she went into the lorry with her horse. As soon as they were up there, literally straight away, she started poking and pushing and hassling the horse to get into the right position where he had to be so she could put the partition across. My heart sank and all I could think was, 'Just a bit of softness for your horse please – that's all he needs right now.' In fact, I did get a tiny bit cross with that girl, and to her credit she listened. 'Let's try to make it nice for him to be with you in that box. How about you just stand there quietly and let him know that it's an OK place to be?' She realized what she had done and started to put things right, but oh my, I sometimes wonder why some horses do anything at all for their owners.

● Find that softness to give to your horse. It is a powerful thing and it will take you a long way. If you can put as much give into this as you extract, then your horse will more than likely go along with your plans. There has to be something in it for him. Find that softness in your hands, when you are leading your horse; find that softness in your hands when you are riding your horse; find that softness in yourself when you are with your horse. Once you see it start to work for you, you will wonder how you managed without it.

So, is softness an elusive thing, gifted only to the supremely talented? Of course not – you can learn it. Take your horse on a lead rope, stand by his side and use the rope to ask him to turn his head towards you. There is a pressure that is so soft he will most likely just move towards it, and there is a pressure above that, which he will resist and that will make him pull the other way. One is an ask and one is a tell, but the important thing is to feel that difference. Your horse will thank you for it.

• • •

Take your horse on a lead rope, stand by his side and use your hand to ask him to move his front feet sideways by touching him on his shoulder. This is a really good exercise that is sometimes very tricky for both the horse and the handler. First try to be as soft as possible in your ask. Nothing may happen, so what I would probably do then is just push a little bit and walk into the horse, which suggests more what you want and means he virtually *has* to move over. As soon as he moves, stop the ask – that is, take off all the pressure and stand quietly. One thing that may happen is that the horse may move forwards or backwards, because moving sideways is quite a tough ask, so I might just adjust my position to show him I don't want forwards or backwards. Keep the whole thing as low key as possible – when a horse is being asked for something but he doesn't know what it is, he can find it highly stressful. If you show the horse at this point that you have patience and understanding, you will almost certainly get a result.

Once you get your first sideways step and reward it with a release, the next ask will probably be easier for your horse. As soon as it is clear that your horse understands what you want, then work on softening up your asks. Over a few days you should be able to move your horse in a nice circle on his haunches by just using really soft asks and giving really good releases. My aim here would be to achieve all of this with little or no stress to the horse.

Some of you may try this and find it really hard. It's quite difficult to put things like this into words, because often things happen that you don't expect and then you find that those eventualities haven't been covered in the instructions. I'm sure we've all been there. If it doesn't work out for you, don't worry. The importance of all this is not so much in the detail of the exercise, it's more in the sentiment. This is no more than a small exercise to prove to you that softness can work for you and your horse.

# Why no stress?

Think about the exercise above. There is a crucial part in it where you are trying to explain to the horse what it is that you want. The horse knows that you are asking for something because he feels the ask, but as yet he hasn't worked out what exactly it is that you want. He may try forwards and he may try backwards, but then he realizes that neither of those tries releases the ask, so then he has to think, 'What else could it be?' Your position and pressure at this crucial point can really help the horse to work out what it is that you want from him.

When horses are asked for something, it is in their nature to try to find that thing and give it to you. You could look at this in a sort of spiritual way and say that it is because there is some kind of special relationship between the horse and the human, or you could be more down to earth and say that it is simply because horses will look for whatever they need to do to find the easiest way out of a situation (what renowned American horse trainer Ray Hunt calls a 'bind'). I tend towards the latter, but who knows and does it matter? What we have to realize is that, to some degree, to a horse pressure equals stress, and that is what the horse is motivated by – he needs to relieve himself of that stress.

So why should we try to work without stress, or rather with a minimum of stress? Well, do you want your horse to associate you with stress? Of course not – we've all seen sour horses and they're not sour for no reason. I was watching a trainer trying to teach his horse to move backwards. He achieved his goal no problem and the horse was almost running back from just a raised finger in no time at all. But I found the way that he did it was not so pretty. He asked the horse to move back by using his finger in a repetitive pointing motion aiming between her eyes. It was quite clear that she had no idea what he wanted but she soon found out, because on the count of three he whacked her on the front of the neck with the coils of his rope and she flew back in shock. Next time she saw that finger she was right on her toes, anxious to get it right before she got whacked again.

I watched for a bit longer and the same method was used to move the mare sideways. It was a case of 'Get it right, buster, or something's going to happen that you don't like.' I came away in turmoil, because I began to wonder if maybe my horses weren't as sharp as they could be because I was too soft on them. But one thing is for sure – I've got to be comfortable with what I'm doing, and personally I'm not comfortable with those methods. I need to know in my own mind that I'm being fair to my horses: that's the relationship I want with them. Maybe they will be a bit slower on the uptake, but if that's the case, then that's the price I will have to pay.

Let's just think about this a bit more. When you ask a horse for something and he doesn't understand what you want, and you increase the pressure because he's not doing what you want, what he's experiencing is an increasing urgency to find a way out of the increasing pressure. If he then stands there still thinking about things and you increase the pressure some more, eventually he's going to take a stab at finding a way out. It may be that you will get lucky and you will get what you want, but in extremis it may be that your horse might say something along the lines of, 'No way, I can't cope with this, I've got to find some way out of here, maybe I'll try a rear, and if that doesn't work, maybe I'll throw in a few bucks.' That probably will work for your horse in terms of releasing the pressure, so now you've trained yourself a horse who every time he gets asked to do something that he doesn't understand, or something he doesn't want to do, knows exactly how to get out of that ask – a quick rear and a few bucks and the problem's gone.

Now I'm not saying that training horses using this method is wrong, or that it causes bucking horses – obviously not, it's extremely popular and there are lots of horses trained in this way going around no problem at all. All I'm saying is that it doesn't suit me. If I want to increase the pressure, which for sure I often do, I try to combine it with even more effort from myself to show the horse what it is that I want him to do. The higher we raise the stakes, the more stress we cause and the less our horse will want to know about us in the future. If we keep it sweet with our horse then it gets to a point where when we ask for something new, there is no tension or stress in the horse at all because he has been there loads of times before and he knows nothing bad is coming next. He knows all he has to do is find what we want and so he's only too happy to look for it.

I'm going to repeat myself again here, but it's important. If I need to up the pressure, if I can I do it in a way that helps my horse understand the way out of it. For example, if I want to move my horse backwards and he doesn't get it when I put a little ask on the halter rope, then I might up the pressure a tad on the rope and at the same time walk towards him so that he almost has to take a backward step. As soon as he even begins to *think* backwards, then I will release all the pressure and he will soon work out what I want. As soon as I can, I'll get back to soft – it just works so well.

## Do you like your horse?

I know it might sound odd, but you're going to find all this much easier if you do like your horse. Or do you just like what he can do for you, or even perhaps what you fantasize he can do for you? If this is the case, a lot of what I'm talking about may not make much sense to you.

If you truly like your horse, you will truly want to be nice to him. Or, to put it in more horse-trainer-speak terms, you will truly want to get things right for him. In the past I have often come into the house after working with a horse and said something along the lines of, 'I really don't like that horse, I really can't see what so and so sees in him.' I'm a bit wised up to that one now, though, because I've worked out that that kind of sentiment is really code for 'I'm really struggling to get some communication going between me and this horse'.

When Apollo first came to our yard, I really didn't like him. I liked the look of him: he is a huge, and I mean huge, blue Belgian working horse. His head alone is almost the size of a Shetland pony. The thing was that he just wasn't interested in people, and although he got on with his work, it was all done with a feeling of slight reticence. He had got a bit used to pushing his weight around and people were forever pushing him around in return. He didn't think a lot of human beings; he almost just saw them as irritants. It took me several days to get to like that horse and I remember the actual moment when it happened. I was standing with him in the yard and there was a fair bit going on around the place, and I just started scratching him around his neck. He showed me that he appreciated what I was doing and the whole thing turned into one of those scratchy sessions that horses just love, and from then on we started to get along OK. Nothing had changed except that we had a bit of first-class communication together, and that was all it took. I got a bit more gentle and I gave him a bit more respect and now we like each other fine.

Since then I've really started to notice that every time I go out on a job and meet a new horse, there seems to be a point where we suddenly warm to each other and I start to say things like, 'Oh, what a beautiful horse.' Now I am starting to realize that there are no unbeautiful horses, there are just horses that so far I have failed to get on with.

All that aside, it is quite obvious that your feelings towards your horse will influence the way you behave around him. I was watching a lady riding her horse and she was a good rider. Well, I guessed she was a good rider because she had worked in some top yards up and down the country. She was struggling a bit with her turns on the forehand and I couldn't help noticing that she was using her legs pretty heavily. It wasn't my job, so I just stood and watched, and what I saw was that over and over it looked like the goal of turning on the forehand had become more important than the softness between her and her horse. Now I know this is easy to say and it can make me sound very good, saying it, but I also know how easy it is for me to go down this very same road. How easy it is to stand there and say to yourself, 'Huh, I can do turn on the forehand, she just needs a bit more feel; no wonder the horse is fighting against her.' But you know what's coming next when you start to think like that. You're going to be on a horse and you're going to ask him for a sideways step and he's going to show you that you're no different from the next man (or woman). And this is the important thing – and I know there will never be any scientific proof either way on this one because it's probably beyond science – my advice to everyone who works with horses is to approach the job with some humility and a small amount of 'unknowing'. In the end it might just come down to pressure – the pressure of your knowledge and expectations can sometimes make you try to force a result that might come so much more easily if you were a little less 'there' in your head and little more 'there' in your heart.

## Can horses feel the 'unknowing'?

When I talk about the 'unknowing' here, I'm talking about a place within yourself where you know nothing. It's an experience beyond the logic and understanding of your mind. This is the place you are when you are in the moment, just getting on with your life without thinking about it. It's very peaceful and without conflict.

To do the job with Cruse, the bucking horse, I needed a rider. Vicky lives about three miles away. I've known her for years, and I knew that she got on 'dodgy' horses. I guess that because we came from such different backgrounds in terms of horses I had never thought of working with her. Anyway, I was invited to do a little demo for a local riding club. It was an interesting evening for many reasons, but the next day Vicky came around to say how much she had enjoyed watching me work. I took my chance and asked her if she would help me with Cruse and she was happy to give it a go.

I had a few ideas about bucking horses that I wanted to try out so, once Vicky had agreed to help, there was a big part of me that wanted to say yes to the job, and that's what I did. I had read an almost throwaway line in a book about how to work with bucking horses. The advice was this: check that the horse is really soft to move his feet in every direction before you even consider getting on him. I could see the logic in this, especially with Cruse because he was fine with the rider until you asked him to move and then that first step seemed to be the trigger that sent him into orbit. Horses don't like to lose their balance, it feels unsafe, and with some their reaction to this insecurity is to buck. I worked on the ground with Cruse for the first few days getting him to move around forwards, backwards and sideways to my asks, and I also worked in the round pen getting him to move away from me softly in walk and trot without any anxiety. My plan was that just a small ask from me on the ground would move him off with the rider on in just the same way. Once he had seen that he could do it with no problem, then hopefully things would start to fall into place for him.

Well, the day came and we put Vicky on and it all went exactly how we wanted it to. A few days later it was Faye, the owner's, turn. Cruse was in the stable and he was working through a few things. He had come to us with a lot of problems about having a rider on his back and over the past few days things had changed a lot for him. Now he could walk and trot around the sand school with a rider, and he'd also been on a short hack. Today was the day when Faye had come up for her first ride and she was understandably concerned. Bar one, every time when she had ridden him before she had ended up on the floor pretty quickly. On the one occasion she had stayed on, she had ridden through a fairly hectic rodeo session before he calmed down and accepted the situation.

I could see that Faye was a bit nervous and I thought she might as well get right in there before she thought too much more about it,

'She went into the stable and Cruse turned his back on her and
wouldn't let her catch him. This is something that happens a lot when
horses are working through things in their minds — they just get fed
up with the hassle of it all and would rather be left alone.'

so I asked her to tack up Cruse ready to go. She went into the stable and he turned his back on her and wouldn't let her catch him. This is something that happens a lot when horses are working through things in their minds – they just get fed up with the hassle of it all and would rather be left alone.

I watched for a few seconds as Faye tried to work out what to do, which was not easy for her because all the emotional stuff was kicking in about why Cruse was doing this to her. I decided pretty quickly to get in there and help, and this is what I mean about the 'unknowing'. I could have tried to tell Faye what to do to try to get Cruse on her side, but the trouble was I didn't know myself, so telling Faye was going to be difficult. I knew that having a horse stuck there in confusion about whether to be caught or not was not what we wanted, so I went into the stable and quietly walked up to him and clipped on the lead rope. Why did he let me do that? Could it have been that I wasn't thinking about it, I was just there in the moment, without a plan? All I had was the feel between me and him.

Of course, there are so many other factors in this equation that it isn't possible to work out what really happened there, but I do think that sometimes things work better when we don't think about them too much. There seems to be a higher plane of consciousness that is more efficient than the level of the thinking mind, and I'm pretty sure that horses appreciate it and can pick up on it very easily. At the same time, I think it is important to understand that we can't just bumble through life without thinking about it – that could well be the road that leads to chaos. That higher consciousness is something that is there for us human beings to experience though. I have a friend who is a mountaineer and he talks about 'being in the zone' where he can just climb without thinking, and how much more efficient his climbing is when he is in this space. It's the same thing, isn't it? I'm sure that good riders know that too. Beyond the hubbub of our thoughts, there is a harmony that feels good – good to us and good to our horses.

# What do you want from your horse?

I have talked a lot about what horses need from humans – it's pretty straightforward and doesn't vary much, if at all, from horse to horse. How about looking at things from the horse's point of view and listening to the question that he is asking: 'What do you want from me?' Some horses find it hard to get an answer to this question. The humans they have to deal with range in a spectrum from completely scatty through average and then on through to very organized and methodical in their responses. The horses with the completely scatty owners soon realize that they aren't really getting any answers to their questions, and many give up even trying to find them; the lucky ones end up making the best of it and getting on with their own lives. Of the horses belonging to the middle range of owners, some will find a way through and be fine, and others will not be able to cope too well. But the horses with the organized and methodical owners will most likely be able to relax and enjoy their lives in the knowledge that they can work out and provide, or at least have a go at providing, what their owners are after.

Beyond the immediate requirements that they have to provide for us, such as basic manners around the yard and so on, for most horses things move on into the real serious world of horsemanship. Here they are often expected to win prizes for racing or jumping, or for successfully pulling off tricky manoeuvres, or in some cases they even have to compete for prizes handed out based on the way they look. When you look at the horse's lot like that it really does start to seem a bit bizarre, doesn't it? We actually co-opt horses into our human world and get them involved in things that no way on earth would they ever do in their horse world, and we ask them to compete for values that are worth absolutely nothing to them. I don't have a problem with any of this, by the way, but I do think that we need to be very careful not to put all of our needs completely before those of the horse.

Anything we ask of our horse needs to be done with us being fully conscious of its effects on the horse. We need to be careful that we are not causing damage to our horse's well-being through trying to fulfil our own dreams. In the end, this is a personal judgement that we all have to make, and of course, what each person decides to do with their horse is their business, not mine. But this train of thought has led me to a point where when I ask my horse to do something for me, I want him to be happy to do it. If, within those parameters, I can go for a day-long ride on the moor, or I can pick up a few prizes or a bit of recognition, well that's a bonus and that's great.

In the great scheme of things, for me all those things are pretty meaningless compared to the joy of owning a happy horse.

## The wrong horse

A man is sitting near a well watching the world go by. It is a beautiful day and another man comes walking along. He is ecstatically happy. He has just proposed to his beautiful girlfriend and she has accepted his proposal, but in his happiness he is not paying attention to where he is walking and he falls into the well.

Now, whose fault is it that the man fell into the well? Is it the fault of the man who built the well and didn't put a fence around it? Or maybe it's the fault of the man who was sitting nearby minding his own business – he could have warned the guy that he was dangerously close to the well. Or is it the fault of the man who fell down the well, because his mind was on other things and he wasn't paying attention?

• • •

There was a survey done recently in which one-third of the people who had recently bought a horse admitted that they thought they had bought the wrong one for them. It's no easy task buying the right horse, and when you buy the wrong one it's no easy task sorting out what to do next.

Owning a horse is not like owning something that can't be changed. At least if you get things slightly wrong when you buy your horse, you can work on the issues and hopefully make progress towards your goal. For a lot of owners, this is part of the joy of owning a horse – it's a project.

But what about when you get it totally wrong, and who is going to be responsible for the small number of horses that simply cannot cope with the constraints we ask them to put up with? One of the first jobs I got called out to do was for a small girl called Wendy who had bought a big hairy cob that she called Brihte, which apparently is Irish for 'trousers' – it was all to do with the huge amount of feather on his legs that made him look as if he was wearing flares.

I'm sure Wendy won't mind me saying that she was more or less a beginner. She had had a horse on loan for a while and decided that she was ready to own one. Brihte was just up the road and was in a bit of trouble already, and Wendy went to see him. He had recently been imported from Ireland by a dealer and was now in the hands of a couple of young girls who were terrified of him. His problem – and this is the bit that people were missing – was that he was absolutely petrified of just about everything to do with humans. So a lot of what he did was quite dangerous, like wheeling around to get away, or taking off at the slightest opportunity, or cow kicking with his back feet.

Wendy bought this horse because she felt sorry for him, and in all truth she couldn't really have bought herself a more inappropriate one. She had arranged to keep him at livery in a small yard, where he was immediately banned from living with other horses because he was 'dangerous'. He very quickly got a reputation that was about as far away from the truth as it could possibly have been, and when I got to the yard to see him he was all on his own tethered up in a tiny paddock.

Looking back now on how I approached this job, I feel quite sad. In all innocence, I truly believed at that time that you could go along and see a horse, show it a few things and hey presto, everything would be fine. I worked with Wendy and Brihte for a couple of sessions and left her with a few exercises to do in between times, and I genuinely thought that things would come right for them both. I guess now I would be a bit more realistic and perhaps would have spotted that the difficulties were in a bit deeper than that, and that Brihte's behaviour was due to a tad more than just a slight misunderstanding.

A few days after my second visit Wendy was on the phone. Brihte had to leave the yard because the other owners couldn't cope with the chaos he was causing. Could I go and pick him up and have him at my place for a while? When I got there, Brihte was in a stable and it took me 20 minutes to get near enough to him to put on his halter – at one point I was right by him and someone across the yard shouted at their horse and Brihte shot off across the box as if a gun had been fired by his ear. I eventually got hold of him and led him out into the yard and towards the lorry. Remember that at the time I had only been working as a so-called horse trainer for a few weeks and I felt very conscious of the need to succeed at what I was doing – nowadays, for good or bad, I'm not under so much pressure.

As I walked to the lorry, I could see all these eyes watching and waiting for Brihte to show me what was what. I got to the ramp and he was still with me. It felt good and I just went for it. 'Come on boy,' I muttered under my breath. Up we went and there we stood, in the

'As I walked to the lorry, I could see all these eyes watching and waiting for Brihte to show me what was what. I got to the ramp and he was still with me. It felt good and I just went for it.'

lorry. I called Wendy to stand with him while I shut the ramp and then we were on our way.

I could write a book about Brihte. Five years later and he's still here at our place. We changed his name to Brixton, because it suits him better – he looks as though he should be pulling a milk cart in 1930s London. We worked with him for a while with the idea that Wendy would have him back, but, all credit to her, she realized he was not the right horse for her, and in the end she just asked us if we wanted him. We didn't really – why on earth would anyone want him? He's not a lot of use: something so bad has happened to him that he just can't forget it, and when people are around he's always on edge, worrying about what's coming next. Looking after Brixton is my contribution to the needy horses in this world. I very much doubt it was his fault he got into the mess he's in, so as long as we're doing horses, he can stay with us.

Wendy got real about Brihte. He took up a few months of her life while she worked out the best way forward. She felt the responsibility that she had as the owner of the horse, but she also realized that they were totally wrong for each other. She did get lucky in a way, in that she found him a new home she was happy for him to go to. It's not always that easy. Many owners soldier on with 'the wrong horse' because there is often nowhere else for that horse to go. Some horses just can't fit into the human way of things, they are just too damaged and too difficult, some get lucky and find some space somewhere to live out their lives.

I guess because of the nature of our business, we come across these difficult situations now and again. One time I got caught up in a huge debate about a little horse called Splash that belonged to a girl called Lisa. Splash was very nappy and could rear up quite dangerously. I worked with the horse for a couple of weeks and although I thought we could probably have turned her around, I couldn't say that for definite, or even guess how long it would take. In the end, Lisa decided to take Splash home and let her live out the rest of her life as a companion to her other horse. Before this, Lisa had conscientiously worked with Splash for two years and got nowhere with her. There are plenty of other horses out there that would have given Lisa a lot back in return for that amount of effort and commitment, and sometimes difficult decisions have to be made.

## The wrong owner

As soon as anyone makes a rule, especially where horses are concerned, along will come the situation where the rule has to be broken. I say 'has to be broken': I guess nothing 'has to be' anything and I'm sure someone somewhere would have found a different way of doing the job that I did with Robert. But I've often thought about it, because what Sarah and I agreed we had to do was to give him a very stark choice about his biting.

I'm going to say it here, because I don't like pretending: sometimes, with some horses, I take a path that is anything but gentle. I am very aware that there are people who are not happy with any form of confrontation in their work with horses and I don't have a problem with that. But what happens sometimes is that I find myself in a situation where I feel as if I'm moving things backwards instead of forwards. Sometimes it becomes very clear that I am actually teaching the horse to do exactly what I am trying to teach him *not* to do. This often happens on loading jobs, where the horse has learnt from the owner that he really doesn't have to go into the trailer. He gets to a point he is comfortable with and just stands there, and that becomes the routine. I am very keen not to continue down that road, so as soon as I see that kind of syndrome happening I'll do whatever I can to break it up. That might include anything I come up with at the time just to let the horse know that the status quo is no longer an attractive option.

To be blunt, Robert was a young horse who had pretty much been allowed to run the whole show. The first time I worked with him I did a couple of sessions where I tried to show him that life might be better if he relaxed and let me decide on a few things, rather than just controlling everything himself. This was quite a few years ago, and it was at that time that I really started to realize that when things have gone wrong over a period of time it often takes a period of time to put them right. To get to the point, on that occasion, I couldn't help Robert or his owner.

About a year later I had a call from Robert's owner asking if her horse could come to stay, and wondering whether during his stay we could put a saddle and rider on him. At the time I was pleased to get a second chance to work with Robert – the first time around it felt like leaving unfinished business, and more than anything I wanted to see if I could set up some kind of working relationship between me and this horse that would benefit us both.

Never mind putting a saddle and rider on Robert: I kid you not, if you or anyone or anything else like a rope or rein was within two feet of his mouth he would bite it, and no matter what you did he would bite it again, and again, and again, and forever. It was truly astounding how persistent he was – he was in fact completely and utterly addicted to biting and that was that. If you have come across bitey horses, you may have found that one thing that doesn't seem to work particularly well is fighting back. A lot of horses take that as a challenge and come back even more, and this was definitely the case with Robert.

At this point, if any of you are thinking along the lines of, 'Shouldn't you work on the relationship?' and so on, I'm completely with you; after all, it is my approach of choice every time. But in this case, things were a bit more drastic and after a few days, and some

*'I took up the long lines and Sarah put on a thick coat and went up front, and
we set off with Robert around the pen.'*

discussion with Sarah, I decided to go in 'all guns blazing' and try to free this young horse from his deadly habit.

We planned to long line Robert in the round pen, but he was so distracted by the long lines within his biting zone that it was only possible to long line him if someone was leading him round too. Of course, they and their rope then became a biting target as well. It was very sad to watch. I took up the long lines and Sarah put on a thick coat and went up front, and we set off with Robert around the pen. Every single time he went to bite, I just took up a hold on the opposite rein with the exact same pressure that he was using to bite, so that the pay-off for his efforts was a niggling jerk in the opposite direction to his bite. It was a good system, because if and when Robert didn't bite then he got a bit of peace from the opposite rein. We worked in walk for 20 minutes at a time, two sessions a day, and by the third day we were beginning to wonder if we might have to come up with something else. You can imagine all the thoughts that went through our heads, along the lines of 'Are we being fair to this horse?'. But then suddenly we got a small breakthrough – Robert missed a beat and walked for a few yards without a bite. A few moments later he completed his first quarter lap in peace, and from there over the next few days he began to leave his biting behind him.

Robert turned into a sweet horse very quickly and became extremely pleasant to be with. He knew no fear, which is often the case with serious biters, so in some aspects he was easy to work with – we had the rider on in no time and he took it all in his stride.

Robert isn't the only horse that I have confronted head-on – sometimes I really do feel that it is best to get on in there and sort things out rather than maybe mess about for months. Three years of biting and the consequent appalling relationships with people, and the prospect of a lifetime of being hit and screamed at, were all sorted out in three hard days. It's got to be worth it, hasn't it?

● There's something we have to realize about horses and that is that they are fine until they meet humans. I have worked with quite a few horses that have bad behavioural problems and in a lot of cases I have got results I am really pleased with. But horses are not like machines that you just mend and send back and they continue to work fine. No, these horses get sent back, often into the very circumstances that caused the problems in the first place, and what happens? Often all the problems simply come flooding back.

At some point, if you are the owner of a horse, then you have to take responsibility for his well-being. It's your horse, and if he bites you then you cannot blame him – all your horse is doing is filling the space you are leaving him. Of course, this is an extreme statement. You know and I know that if your horse has a vice like weaving, say, then it is unlikely that any amount of work by you will help him to sort out that particular problem. But extreme statements need to be made, because to the horse no excuses are acceptable. To a horse, if things aren't good enough then they aren't good enough and problems will occur.

Horses need the best, especially horses that have low tolerance levels for less than 100 percent care in their handling. It doesn't take much to throw some horses off balance in terms of behaviour, and that cuts both ways. Sometimes a minor change in the handling can cause a dramatic improvement, but conversely a minor change in the wrong direction can make things go the other way just as drastically too.

Why am I saying all this? Because I know that Robert went back home and started biting again, and that makes me sad. It didn't have to be like that. It looked as if the job we did didn't work, but it did. There was nothing wrong with Robert – he just couldn't cope with too much slack.

# Give your horse what he needs

I was listening to an expert on the radio talking about human body language, and one of the questions he was asked was whether he could look at a group of people and pick out the potential leader. One of the strong pointers he said he would look for was quietness. Now, I'm not saying that we should all go around being quiet, or for that matter that we should all go around trying to be the leader. For me, when I'm in a group of people, in a lot of cases I am more than happy to be led anyway, as long as I am comfortable with the direction that the leader is taking me.

But when it comes to your horse, he does want a leader and if you want to be that leader then you need to come up with the qualities your horse is looking for. Again, I'm not saying that you need to be quiet or do nothing, but it really does help your horse make his decisions if he can weigh you up without too much trouble, and that means he needs to see that what you do makes sense to him. So when I say 'nothing', you can look on it in a 'deep' way if you like, because it works that way for me too, but really it's about not adding in a load of stuff you don't need.

Sometimes when I watch people working with their horses I can't help wondering what the horse makes of everything that is going on. Some of the things the horses are asked to do over and over again, often with the asking being done in an extremely crude way, must make no sense at all to them. We watched a girl putting her horse through a little programme of schooling exercises the other day, and halfway through she asked Sarah why she thought the horse was getting so cross with the whole thing. My wife explained that if she wanted to get the horse on her side, then maybe one thing she could try was to give the exercises some meaning to the horse. For example, if you walk your horse up to a gate, open it, walk through, turn around and shut the gate, you and your horse will do at least four of the movements the girl was looking for in her exercises – walking forward, stopping, backing up, turning on the forehand, and possibly turning on the haunches – and all for a reason that your horse can understand.

It's a subtle line that we have to draw, because ultimately there may be no real reason for the horse to open and shut the gate, but we can make him think that there is. Far better to achieve our aims this way than to bully him into performing all these actions purely because he knows that if he doesn't he will get a stick and a rope waved in his face.

• • •

There is a section in the *Bhagavad Gita* where Arjuna asks Krishna how we can live in this world taking the path of inaction, when clearly our very existence means that we have to act. Now, I'm no Hindu scholar and there is a very good chance that I've got this completely wrong on every level, but it makes perfect sense to me. (I'd better just point out that the copy of the *Gita* that I read, and have since lost, was apparently not a good translation, so what with that and then my take on it, plus the fact that I read it a good few years ago, this is probably a million miles from what is actually said.) What I got from it was this: if we can act in this life from a state of consciousness beyond the mind, focused on our higher self, then those actions will be free. I've also put my liberal interpretation on to this to suit my needs, as we do, and what I've come up with is that if I act in good faith in this life then I cannot do wrong and I cannot be open to criticism and blame. Sure, I can make mistakes, get things wrong and cause chaos, and people will have a go at me, but where it counts for me, in my heart, I know I've tried my best and I can feel peace within. Oh, if only life was so easy!

So, this is also how it has to be for the horse. He needs to have a reason for doing all this stuff, and that reason can be respect for and trust in you. He needs to know that if he tries his best he is beyond blame. He needs to know that if things go wrong you will be there to help him through. He needs to feel safe, just as we do.

# Sometimes Things Go Your Way

· · · · · · · · · · · · · ·

A long time ago, my brother and I owned a small herd of cows and ran a little milk round selling bottled unpasteurized milk. It was a tough way to make ends meet – if I'm honest, the ends didn't actually meet, but we managed to fill our bellies so it couldn't have been that bad. Then one year the summer was really hot and it didn't rain for weeks. All the grass turned brown and the milk yields went right down. I was only a young man and I carried the weight of the world on my shoulders a bit more than I do now. I felt responsible for getting that milk out there and I worried about letting our customers down.

Things got so bad that in the end we started taking the cows out onto the road to graze the hedgerows and verges. This helped keep things going for a little while longer. One evening I went out into the yard and looked down the field, and I couldn't see the cows anywhere. I rushed up to the gate just in time to see them walking up the drive towards the road. They had managed to push the gate open and had decided to take the grazing situation into their own hands. Dusk was falling and I was all on my own with this one; I had to get those cows back before it got dark.

I rushed ahead of them to try and turn them before they reached the grass but they were in a determined mood. I managed to grab a stick out of the hedge on my way, but compared to the prospect of the lush verges the stick was meaningless to those hungry cows. I desperately tried to turn them back, but as I held one side of the drive one or two cows would try to take me on the other. I was at my absolute limit as I tried to prevent a mass breakout. As I ran from one side of the track to the other and the cows began to realize that they had me pretty stretched, I had one of those kind of 'cosmic' moments where I suddenly saw, with some clarity, my position in the creation. Me, this small being, one of billions, on a small patch of this world, desperately trying against all the odds to exert some control over this universe. If those cows wanted to go past me, they could. I was at their mercy.

I had to try to get a result. Giving up was not an option. In the end, I managed to get the message across to all but one of the cows. That left me and one very determined old cow, facing each other right at the gateway. I knew if she got past me I would lose the whole herd. She went from one side to the other and I knew that if she only realized it, I had no hope of stopping her. I looked at her eyes, she was a beautiful animal. We were both trapped together in that moment and our minds and desires were set in opposite directions. I saw my destiny was completely in the hands of fate. I didn't pray as such, but I did realize that the choice was no longer mine. We stood for a second longer and she softened, turned and slowly walked back down the drive away from the grass.

I felt as if something had shown me some mercy. I also know that those kinds of feelings - indeed, all the feelings that I had been through in that short time - were the natural result of all the events I had just experienced. I'm not looking to hang a load of meaning on any of it - I try not to do that; I'm just saying that sometimes it looks as if we are in control when in reality we're not. In some ways, the only tool in our box really is a prayer.

# The real world: finding the key

*I know I am not alone in my search for the key to improving my horsemanship. In fact, over the last 20 years or so the number of horse owners on this quest has created quite an industry in the western world. Now there are even books being written encompassing all the different methods and techniques we can all try in our desire to get better results from our horsemanship. And, as in life itself, sometimes the search can become more of a focus than finding the answer.*

It is difficult, if not impossible, to write anything definitive on this subject, because the fact is that we all want different things from our horses. The results that satisfy me, and the way I go about getting them, will quite likely be very different to those that satisfy the next person, and it is surely everyone's privilege to pursue whichever path they choose with their horses, as it is with everything else in their lives.

But whichever method or technique you choose to try out or pursue, there are some things in common, if not to all, then certainly to most of them. You will see good horsemen throughout the entire spectrum of horsemanship, whether it is on one of the most far-out weekend courses you could ever find, or just down at your local village show.

As I've said already, I'm not over-keen on systems of training that bat on and on, drilling horses to do things that mean nothing to them. I understand what these systems are designed to achieve, or at least I think I do – they are looking to make the horse into a soft, compliant animal that always gives when asked. Some people, in their wisdom, have analysed the movements that horses make in the herd and what they mean, and through this analysis they have formulated a programme to achieve similar communication through reproducing these movements – for example, getting the horse to move diagonally back and away from you signifies to the horse that you are the more powerful half of the partnership. I'm not saying that this system is correct or not, or that it is good or bad – what I am saying is that it can be both. What is important is that if you decide to follow any method of training at all, it really needs to be done with sensitivity, and that means in empathy with your horse's situation. If you work your horse sympathetically, taking care of his state of mind, making sure that he is giving you what you want willingly, not reluctantly, and keeping him happy, then you are getting something right.

What often happens with systems and methods is that the larger goal of achieving a willing horse gets sacrificed for the smaller goals of completing the exercises. Of course, there is always the belief that if you just keep batting away at something then sooner or later the horse is bound to just give in and get on with it, and to a degree I think this can sometimes be true. But you just need to be careful that you don't set off other issues in the process.

# Taking responsibility – Cruse continued

Remember Cruse, the bucking horse? After Vicky had ridden him for me, and then we had put Faye on him too, things were looking good. I was pleased because, as I have already said, it was a job that I didn't really want to do, partly because I was so busy with other things but also because of the percentage thing. Those kinds of jobs have a small chance of success and consequently a high chance of failure. What I always say to the client before I start is that, no matter what, I will try my best.

We just needed a few more days to get Faye hacking out and Cruse really sure in his new-found confidence. And then, out of the blue, Faye announced that she was taking Cruse home because she felt she was losing touch with him. I was lost for words and just went along with it, only managing to say, in a fairly humble way, that I thought both Cruse and Faye could do with a bit more time really, but never mind, if they couldn't manage it, good luck.

As the days went by things moved on, and then Faye got on the phone again. She wanted me to go down and help her with Cruse. I picked up Vicky on the way, thinking that everything would be how it was when we had last seen Cruse a couple of weeks before. But when we got there and I started to work with him, it was chaos. When I eventually did put the saddle on Cruse, he bucked like I had never seen him buck before. He was like a different horse, in fact he was worse than the very first day he had arrived at my place the first time around. There was no way I was going to put a rider on that horse, so I decided we should do a bit of long lining and see how things went.

After a few minutes of fairly tight work (that means work that was not full of holes), Cruse was beginning to get back to how I liked him, really relaxing and happy to go with my asks. I probably could have put Vicky on there and then, but in the great scheme of things I felt it was more important to find out why Cruse had drifted so far away over the past fortnight, and whether Faye had what it takes to get him back if it happened again. This is what I mean about responsibility – Faye was not taking it, and Cruse was having to carry more of a load than he could handle. Admittedly, I was a bit cross, and as I left I told Faye that she seriously needed to consider whether she was up to the standard that this horse required. I might have been a bit rude, but she took it well.

'As I write this, Cruse and Faye are a job in progress. But for me it has really helped to make a few things clear. You cannot bail out on your horse – you have to take the responsibility or he will have to take it for himself, and horses aren't so good at that.'

A few days later and Faye was on the phone again. She had decided that she wanted to continue the work with Cruse and could I do a session with them. Off I went to see if I could sharpen up Faye's groundwork and, blow me, I was in for a shock. Gone was the sloppy person who argued my every point. Here was a horsewoman I could work with. We had a great hour of Faye working like a pro, and Cruse was as happy as anything. When Faye made the odd mistake, she was right in there dealing with it – no longer was she just bailing out and leaving Cruse to sort it out, and then beating herself up for being no good – it was good work and I came away feeling inspired.

As I write this, Cruse and Faye are a job in progress and who knows which way it will go. But for me it has really helped to make a few things clear. You cannot bail out on your horse – you have to stay in there with him, taking the responsibility or he will have to take it for himself, and horses aren't so good at that. Their responses aren't always to our liking. Clarity of responsibility is what the horse needs and blurred edges don't work so well. I sometimes think of it like this: I decide where we go and how fast, and you take us there. Stick to that and it will be fine for both of us.

## Finding your confidence

Of course, it is all very well to bang on about 'do this, do that'. It's not always that easy, is it? Sometimes we can understand the theory but simply do not have the confidence to put it into practice.

Number one rule for me here is to work within the levels I am comfortable with. A few weeks ago I was working with our new young colt to get him ready for the farrier. When we bought him I don't think his feet had ever been touched. The front nearside was really splayed out flat and had a big split in it, and the others weren't that much better. I realized that it was probably because he was not too happy about having people around his feet that the job had been left. I wasn't over-concerned, because I felt confident I could soon sort this out and start to work towards getting him right again.

I did the front feet okay. He was a bit unsettled and wary of me, but he let me trim them up a bit so I was pleased with that. When I started on the back feet he was quite worried but I pressed on, and then all of a sudden he jumped forward and I somehow got dragged underneath him. As he tried to get away from being on top of me, he caught my jaw with his back foot and knocked me for six. I got up, stumbling about in a total state of shock. Thankfully I was physically fine, but the aftermath of the incident was that I had a real problem about going near his back feet.

Over the last few years I have worked with many people who have 'lost their bottle' around horses, and I have carefully gone back to a point that they are comfortable with and rebuilt their confidence at a speed with which they can cope. It is interesting work, because it is not always about dealing with rational thoughts and arguments. It is often a matter of waiting for something inside the person to click back into place, so it is very important not to risk replicating the situations that have triggered off the problem in the first place. It's exactly the same situation with a horse – if you have a horse that has problems with gates because he has been caught in a dodgy narrow gate, you wouldn't go back and risk it happening again. You would begin to rebuild his confidence by starting work with a good, sound, wide gate. The job would be to show the horse that gates are okay and not to reinforce his idea that they are dangerous.

Back to me and my young colt. The difficulty was that we started out in a situation where it was just him that was worried about his back feet and I wasn't worried at all, and we ended up in a situation where both of us were in a state about it. Not ideal, because horses like to feel confidence around them, not nervousness. So many times I have been out to see people's horses and been able to do stuff with them that they couldn't do, just because the horse could feel that I was confident in what I was doing. And now here I was in the exact same boat as the people I had been working for.

I knew this job was about working on myself, and in truth that is what this whole job with horses is about for everyone else, too. At the point when you realize that *you* are the main project, then the real work and the real progress begins. When finding that way of being that horses are truly comfortable with becomes your main goal, then things really do begin to fall into place. Truly, if you think you can find a technique or a method that will sort out your horse, and yet you have no desire to make some effort to change yourself to improve things between you and him, then good luck to you – you may well need it.

So, I made a start on rebuilding my confidence. I worked towards getting back to the point where I felt OK about getting in there around the colt's back legs. In my mind I could see that my nervousness and my inability to control it were completely illogical, but that fear was in me really deep. The secret is to take the time that is necessary. Things will come good or not, but there's nothing to gain by rushing in there being the brave hero. That is playing for stakes that are just far too high.

# Rebuilding your confidence

Anne bought Docherty, a nice steady cob, and had lots of fun with him. Then one day something happened, Docherty lost the plot and Anne fell off and got badly hurt. A few weeks later when she had recovered, she was too frightened to get back on to him in case he lost the plot again.

Anne got a friend of ours, Kate, to work with Docherty and to ride him for a while until she felt confident enough to get back on him. Everything was going really well, but Anne could not forget what had happened and it was months before she got to the point where she felt anywhere near happy about the idea of getting back on her horse. This whole thing had turned into a huge deal for her, and after a lot of deliberation she and Kate decided that the best place to carry on the work with Docherty was at my yard. Anne had been here before with him practising her groundwork and felt quite at home.

Here is another really important 'common sense' point about training and working with horses: if you are worried about getting on a particular horse, which would be the better place to do it – in a nice, quiet, small, safe area that the horse was completely familiar with or out in the middle of a 20-acre field? It's obvious, isn't it, so why do we so often make the wrong choices? Working through difficult situations with horses is all about percentages: upping the chances of success and reducing the chances of failure. When people talk about breaking down tasks into smaller pieces, what they are really doing is improving the chances of success. Horses thrive on success – they like to know that they can do things and this gives them confidence. From small successes, confidence grows and can often snowball into big achievements.

And so Anne wanted to get back on Docherty in our round pen where she had worked with him already, in a situation that she had seen he was quite comfortable with. This is good horsemanship, and doubly good considering the state that Anne had got herself into about the whole situation. My wife rode Docherty around the pen for a while and then it was Anne's turn. I have never seen anyone quite so frightened of getting on a horse. She was trying so hard to disguise her fear, but to no avail. However, she was beginning to feel that there would never be a time when she would be truly ready to get back on her horse, and now that she had got as much right as she could, she had to go for it. I held Docherty while Anne mounted and then I led him around the pen for a few circuits in both directions. Anne was really very nervous, but we completed the first part of our maiden voyage without any untoward drama and with Anne's permission I unclipped the lead rope.

Anne rode Docherty around the pen for a couple of minutes, put in a nice halt and asked me to hold him while she got off, which she did successfully. Throughout the whole event Docherty was clearly very aware of Anne's anxiety – you could almost see 'What's wrong?' written across his face. But never mind, the job was done. Anne was safely back on the ground crying her eyes out, and Docherty was on his way back to the stable to stuff his face into his hay.

Now, for those of you who would go around the Grand National course without batting an eyelid, this story might not make the tiniest bit of sense. But that's what it can be like sometimes – I know because I've been there, and coming back is often not so easy. Anne had another ride on Docherty the next day and it was quite a bit easier for her, and now, well, the latest I heard was that the pair of them had done their first dressage test for a couple of years. Patience and care are paying off.

## Trainers, trainers and more trainers

Sometimes when I am working with horses, I look at the people I am working for and wonder if they are wondering how I've got to where I am right now. And sometimes I watch other trainers working and wonder how they have got to where they are, too. Sometimes I listen to people talking about other trainers and I think, 'The work that is going on there right now is the result of all the knowledge that person has, combined with the decisions he is taking right now, in response to whatever responses the horse is making right now. It's the very best that he can do in the situation he is in at this moment.' And for sure you'll always get someone who'll say, 'Oh, that's not how so and so would have done it.' And I think, 'There are people saying that about me when I'm working but really, as true as it probably is, it is a bit of a dumb thing to say. I'm me, not so and so.'

People who put themselves up as horse trainers are there for some reason. They must all be able to do something or they just wouldn't be there. For instance, say you know a trainer who can successfully get a horse around a jump-racing track. How can anyone call that person a bad trainer? Maybe you can call them a trainer who does things in a different way to you, but not a bad trainer. If they were a bad trainer, they wouldn't be in business, because no-one would take their horses to them.

So now I guess I can be accused of supporting all sorts of dodgy training methods, because I've said that if the trainer can get the result the client wants, then they must be a good trainer. I know it's tough, but it's true. However, you have the option – if you want someone to work with your horse, or you want someone to model your horsemanship on, then choose someone who suits you. I don't like the idea of hitting horses, so when I found a trainer who didn't use a stick I watched him to see what I could learn from him. But I also know, from listening to other people, that when they watch the same trainer, they are thinking, 'Oh for goodness' sake, you could sort that out in ten seconds if you'd use a stick.' They can't be saying it for no reason – somewhere along the line something must have happened to give them that idea, so presumably they must have got a good result with a stick in a similar situation.

In the end, what I am saying is let's not be too quick to judge. There are a lot of people out there trying their best and getting a lot right for their customers. But different customers want different things. I've got a good friend who lives in Lambourn, one of the top racehorse areas in this country, and while on a visit to her place we went out on the downs to watch the racehorses training. Some of what we watched was a bit on the wild side, with young horses jumping and bucking about trying to get the hang of cantering up the gallops. On the way home I asked my friend if anyone had considered training the horses in what you might call a more 'natural horsemanship' kind of way. Her answer was brief and to the point. 'Oh yes, people have tried it,' she said, 'round here they're called losers.' It would be nice to think that this might change one day, but I wouldn't put too much money on it myself – maybe horses run faster if you keep them a little bit on the wild side.

• • •

I sometimes go to this place called the Natural Health Centre in a nearby town. As you go in through the front door there is a huge noticeboard on the wall facing you and it is completely covered with different posters all offering either cures or wisdom to help you on your way through life. When I see it I often think, 'I really hope I don't get cancer, because I wouldn't have a clue which one of these guys to choose to help me cope with it.' Then you go through the next door and there on the left is another whole wall covered with a whole load more posters all offering more solutions – by now my mind is boggled and I rush past before my head explodes.

There is an old saying, 'Judge a tree by its fruit', which is a fair enough statement. But sometimes it can be quite a few years before the fruit is ready to try, so this saying is really only of any help to those of us with time on our hands. If your health is going downhill fast, can you really spare the time to work your way through all those different therapies? No way! You're going to take a quick ask around, see if anyone you vaguely respect comes up with any leads, and rush to the nearest person who you think might offer you the best odds of survival. More than likely, in the case of cancer, you'll be off to the doctor's surgery as fast as you can go.

This actually happened to John, a good friend of mine, and sure enough he ended up in the doctor's surgery, only to be told that there was nothing anyone could do for him and his number was up. So off he rushed back to the noticeboard (not the one near me, the metaphorical one called 'the choices in this world'), did a bit of research, and within a fortnight he was on a plane to Mexico. Before you know it he was eating organic carrots and doing coffee enemas for all he was worth. To cut a long story short, many years later and John's still here and still as annoying as ever. He got lucky: he picked the right 'trainer' there, that's for sure. If he'd picked the poster next door, this story might have had a very different ending.

• • •

So there you are with your horse. You don't know much about horses, but one thing you know for sure is that you are having trouble riding him out of the gate. So what do you do? You ask around all the other people in the area to see if they know anyone who can maybe help you with your problem, and that night you get on the phone to your local recommended trainer.

'Yes, no problem, I can sort that out for you,' is just the answer you wanted to hear, and two days later you are dropping your horse off at the trainer's yard.

A couple of weeks pass and you pick up your horse and bring him home, and he's going like a dream. No more questions about whether to go or not – your horse is just push-button. The transformation is unbelievable.

'Wow, that guy is good with horses, that's for sure. I would recommend him to anyone.' And yes, surely we all have to agree, you picked the right trainer there. But what if you'd gone along with one of the other recommendations? It could have worked out there too, or you could have ended up with even more of a problem than you started with, which could lead to you doing the rounds of all the trainers in your area.

● Nowadays, when people ask me what I do, I tell them that I work with horses. Sometimes in the past I called myself a horse trainer, but that just sounds so ridiculous, especially when I think of all the really great trainers that there have been, and all the great trainers that there are, and just how good these people were and are, and just how much they knew and know about every aspect of the horse. But in the end, it doesn't come down to horse trainers, it comes down to you. You are the one who has to make the changes, if you want to improve things with your horse. Long term, horses aren't changed by quick fixes. They can't be, can they, because horses just mirror their situation, so how does a quick fix fit into that?

# All horses are the same (but different)

The nature of every horse is the same. They are driven by the same needs and the same fears. Once you begin to get into their way of thinking, it becomes much easier to work with them. When you meet another person for the first time you have absolutely no idea what is important to them – they are driven by a desire for fulfilment, but the snag is that each person thinks fulfilment comes from different things. It can take anything from a few minutes to a few years to work them out, and sometimes it is impossible. With people, the dreams and desires we have for our lives can be hugely complicated. Fame, fortune, love, sex, security, adventure, power, the quiet life, excitement – the list is almost endless. How these desires get into us no-one really knows, but they're in there, and on top of that we have all our different character traits and moral values multiplied into the equation.

Humans are all uniquely different beings, working our way through from birth to death and trying to make as much sense as we can out of the time we have while we are here on this earth. It's not like that with horses. You meet a horse and you pretty much know what you are getting in terms of responses. What you don't know about is the intensity of the responses. Some horses are much more solid than others; they can cope much more easily when things go haywire. Others have very low tolerance levels and huge reactions, even to the point where they can be totally unworkable.

At one of our workshops we had this big old horse that looked like she had been in a cart before. So we put her in the cart and then someone saw that one tyre was a bit flat. No worries, we'll get it pumped up. As the air was going in, suddenly the tyre burst with an almighty bang like a huge firecracker. This was about two metres behind this horse all strapped up in the cart – it couldn't really have been much worse. The humans were reeling about in shock wondering whether we were all under attack, but bless this old mare, she didn't even flinch. She just stood there as though nothing had happened.

A few years before, I had a little pony that I had bought at the market because my niece was down for a week and she wanted to sit on a horse. The pony was a good solid little Dartmoor-type mare and we did everything we wanted to with her. But the one big mistake we made was that we got a bit over-confident. I had an old cart and I wanted to give it a try, so I long lined the pony around the place, no problem. She then pulled a tyre through the village without putting a foot wrong. I started to think that she had done all this before. I backed her into the shafts, got one side done up and went around to do up the other side. I don't even know what happened next – I think it was when she felt the shaft on her flank, in a split second she was off. The cart was only fixed on one side and as she ran it sort of half tipped up over her back. After about ten metres the shaft broke and she just went. We found the mare about 100 metres away in our back yard with the remainder of the shaft across her back.

*'Suddenly the tyre on the cart burst with an almighty bang, about two metres behind the horse — it couldn't really have been much worse. The humans were reeling about in shock, but bless this old mare, she didn't even flinch. She just stood there as though nothing had happened.'*

You live and learn, don't you? Well, hopefully you do anyway. When I think back now to putting air into that tyre while the cart was attached to that horse, I shiver in my boots.

# Look around you: it's not just horses

Working with horses is a lot to do with bringing your responses in line with theirs, getting in tune with them as quickly as you can, hopefully from the very first moment.

For the last six years, Sarah and I have kept a flock of Whiteface Dartmoor sheep. I've learnt a lot from these sheep and I still do. People say sheep are stupid, but they're wrong. People say that given a choice, sheep will always choose to go the wrong way, and it does look like that sometimes. However, the first thing to learn when dealing with sheep is that they need time to think. You cannot rush them. They are also mega-reactive to every move you make, so if you are heading towards a gate with your flock and you move slightly out of position, you will move your sheep away from the gate. If you then over-react and over-compensate you will probably send them off in all directions, but if you calmly move back on course and give them time, the chances are that they will come back on course too.

When you get to the gate, they might well be concerned about going through it. So, what you mustn't do is stack a load of pressure on them to try to push them through it. If you carefully wait and keep their focus on the gate, the chances are that they will eventually work out that it is safe to go through. It has to be done in their time, when they are ready. Of course, you could try to speed it up but the stakes are high. You might lose the lot of them and have to start all over again, and this time they will trust you even less. It is a delicate balance, working between their conscious, thinking mind and their survival instincts. Sounds familiar, doesn't it?

Over the last six years I have worked hard with my sheep. I have tried to show them that I understand that they need time. They are definitely a calmer flock now than when I first got them, but one thing has never changed and maybe never will. Their propensity to react is as sharp as ever – they'll fire off in a second if I get it wrong. They are food for predators and they really know it. And that sounds familiar too.

• • •

I watched Frank moving his cows about and realized that he was reading them like a book. Perfect pressure-and-release communication that the cows were more than happy with. Plenty of time, waiting for the responses. Clear communication with great care taken not to start off an over-reaction. Nice to watch.

I watched Fred shearing my sheep. It's not an easy thing for a sheep to be turned upside down and have its wool shorn off. Sometimes they think their number is up and struggle in a desperate attempt to save their lives. Fred stays quiet and waits for them to go still before carrying on with the job. Nice to watch.

I watched the guy at the horse market who was on the gate where the horses came into the ring. A really quiet guy dealing with some pretty stressed-out horses. Just gentle movements, opening up the spaces for the horse to walk into. Making it easy for the horse in a difficult situation. Nice to watch.

I watched some guys at the same market trying to load one of their purchases. What a mess the whole thing had got into, as they completely ignored the responses of the pony and the fact that he just needed time. I couldn't watch that for very long. Ugly, so ugly.

You know, in the end I think we can learn from just about everything, because it's all about us, wising up about how things work in this world. The wisdom in some of those farmers, that they were born with or have picked up from working with animals all their lives, is good stuff. We need to get a slice of that; our horses will thank us for it.

# There are some difficult horses

Some horses can never leave their troubles behind. Something has happened to them and it keeps resurfacing in their mind when the going gets tough. These are what people call 'remedial horses'. They are difficult horses to sort out because it's as if their default mode, the one they always return to, is the 'horse with a huge problem'. So, no matter how hard you work to sort things out, and even if you succeed to some degree or other, if you then leave your horse alone even for just a few days, he will revert back to his default mode.

My resident remedial, Brixton, has a real problem with the farrier. If I work really hard with him, I can just about get him to the point where we can put some shoes on him, but by the time that he gets around to needing another set of shoes he's right back to where we started from and totally terrified of the farrier again. It's so hard for him and such a hassle for me that we have decided just to keep him without shoes – luckily he has good feet and it causes no problem at all.

Of course, solutions to remedial problems are not always that easy. Saffron was a young horse that got off to a bad start when her owner tried to take her out riding on her own before she was really ready for the challenge. At the gate Saffron hesitated, and one thing led to another, ending up with Saffron becoming very anxious indeed any time she got anywhere near the gate. Things deteriorated to the point where, rather than go through the gate,

Saffron would rear up really high, frighten the rider and get herself taken back to the yard.

Over the years a lot of work has been put into Saffron, but one thing has never changed: whenever the chips are down and the pressure becomes too much for her, her automatic reaction is to rear. When I first started working with her, even asking her to wait quietly while I tied the gate when getting her in from the field would often cause her to rear. Of course, it's one thing sorting out that kind of behaviour from the ground and quite another sorting it out from on her back. For a rider, it is very difficult to prevent a horse from getting some kind of benefit from rearing. It totally disarms the rider and gives all the power to the horse, which in turn reinforces in the horse's mind the benefit of rearing. So that leaves the best option of finding an answer in working long term on the relationship, to such an extent that the horse feels she no longer needs to find a way out of the situation.

This is challenging and very skilled work which I am confident can lead to successful results. I am committed to the way I work and I have great belief in it. I have no doubt that horses in trouble can be turned around by rebuilding the relationship based on trust. I have seen it work over and over. But sometimes it is a huge commitment that has to be made and the odds are stacked against total success. Think positive is good advice, but you must always be realistic.

## Where to start from

There was once a farmer who had lived on the moor for many years. One day a car pulled up in his yard, and from the look on the driver's face, it was obvious that he was totally lost. The driver wound down the window and greeted the farmer. 'Good afternoon, I wonder if you would be kind enough to tell me how I can find my way to Fernworthy Reservoir?' The farmer thought about it for a few seconds and then he replied, 'Well, kind sir, I know where the reservoir is, that's not a problem. But one thing I would say is, if I was going there I wouldn't start from here.'

That's how I feel about horses, too. Sometimes we know the goal that we want to reach, but we try to get there from the wrong place. When Saffron's owner first rang me for help, she asked me if I could come and ride the horse for her. I don't have a death wish, but even if I did, I wouldn't have started the job from there. Over and over this happens. Someone has a bad loader and as soon as you get to the yard, they start asking what they should do when the horse gets stuck on the ramp of the trailer. Whoa there – let's take a look at how you are with your horse in the stable, and around the yard. Why on earth is he going to follow you into a trailer when he is barely following you across the yard?

> ● Sometimes with really difficult or dangerous horses, we really do have to ask the same question. If you wanted a riding horse, would you start from here? I was once with a guy who was running a clinic and someone in the audience asked him what he would do if he owned a horse that rears. He thought for no more than a second and said, 'I'd sell it.' And he just carried on working as though he'd said nothing, but there's a lot in that answer – it's always stuck with me.

I must get at least one phone call a month from people who want help with rearing horses. It isn't the fault of those horses that they are in the mess they're in: it's all down to people making crucial errors of judgement at crucial times in the work that has been done with those horses. But once it's done it's done and sometimes the damage is in really deep, and – as responsible as we may feel for those horses – human life only comes once to each of us and we should take care of it. If it is we who are causing the same problem over and over, then we are definitely doing something very wrong and we need to take a good hard look at what we are doing. But so often the people trying to sort out the mess are not the people who have caused it – they are well-meaning bystanders who have stepped in to try to make some sense out of some poor horse's life. It's not always so easy.

On an internet discussion group some time ago, someone was wondering what to do about a rearing foal. People were coming on and saying try aromatherapy and try flower remedies, and I was getting very cross about the whole issue. I feel really strongly about this sort of thing, because rearing could become the default mode for that foal quicker than you can imagine. Someone somewhere along the line is going to have a rearing horse. Now if ever there was a chance to take out that rear, surely this has got to be it. I've seen it in one or two of my own foals and dealt with it straightaway – they learn really easily that it is not a good option to take and that's the last you see of it. So that's what I mean when I say that, ideally, I wouldn't start from here: if it's an option, start at the beginning and get it right.

• • •

I have had a few stallions in my care over the last few years, including one I bred from my own mare many years ago. The very easiest one I have had, I bought from the gypsies. He was so good compared to all my others that it was very easy to get complacent and forget that he was a stallion. No way could I ever have done that with any of the others. By the way, I'm not suggesting for one second that getting complacent with a stallion is a good idea. It is a very bad idea. Stallions are horses with a bit more going on, and that bit more is a very powerful thing – you should know that and take account of it.

So, why was Linus such a nice horse to be with? Of course, it is possible he was just born a nice horse, but more likely is that from day one he was brought up to understand how his owners wanted him to behave. Never once in all the time that I had Linus on the end of a rope did he ever even remotely try to do anything other than what I asked him to do. He really made me think about how my horses are, and why. I know the gypsies have reputations for this and that, but I also know that some of those reputations are not always justified. What can't be disputed is that they do know how to get a horse to be how they like them to be. So, whatever techniques they had used to get Linus to be like he was, I bet the one important thing they did was get in there early and nip a few things in the bud.

It's just far easier to set down a behaviour pattern the first time that it happens rather than trying to change it after it has become an established habit. Sometimes with horses it is so tempting to pass over things and 'sort them out later', but it's actually much better for the horse if you sort out 'issues' before they even exist. If I ever breed myself another stallion, I will be looking to get things right from day one.

A common problem that people have with horses is taking one horse away from another when they are really bonded together. This can be a nightmare situation, in that because it is such a traumatic experience to split them up, you put off doing it, and so it compounds itself and just gets even more difficult. This is yet another one of those classic 'I wouldn't start from here' situations, and we have to take the opportunity to learn from this and make sure that we don't let it happen again.

Now, imagine that problem but add in the fact that you are talking about taking a stallion from his herd of mares, or taking a mare out of the stallion's herd. This is a real issue for me, because I have a stallion in with my mares and I am going to need to be able to do these things. I am also going to need to be able to put my mare back in with my stallion.

When I bought Linus, his owner proudly told me that I would be able to do all of those things with no problem. I could also take him out of the field, cover another mare and put him back again. I could also tether him in the field and put in a strange mare. When she came into season she would go over to Linus, he would cover her and the job would be done. I never tried doing those last two things as I didn't need to, but so much of what I had been told about Linus was true that I believe they are true too.

So how did Linus get to be like that? The answer has got to be that very early on, probably from the very beginning, the gypsies showed him that that was how it was and so he just got on with it. He just didn't think or know that it could be any other way. If they had left him a few years and then tried to get him to that point, then they truly wouldn't have had much chance at all.

## It's your choice

Now we are getting to the heart of the matter. If you don't take the important decisions your horse will, and that's where things can start to go a bit off course. Your horse's idea of what needs to happen will almost certainly not be the same as yours. I say 'almost certainly' because it is amazing how many people do get by, to their satisfaction, with a fairly loose arrangement between them and their horse. Go to any local show and you can watch horses and ponies, say, going around quite complicated jumps courses very much to the satisfaction of their riders. All credit to the horses for getting round the course and all credit to the riders for staying on board – something good is going on there. I'd probably be off at the first fence myself, but sometimes it does look a bit like a case of pointing the horse in roughly the right direction and hoping for the best. In terms of being with your horse, a lot of the time, it's not quite the arrangement that I would be after. Who's taking which decisions? That is the crucial question.

• • •

I went back to visit Annabel because her horse was refusing to load again. After my first visit, everything had been fine for a month and then the situation had progressively deteriorated. Annabel called in desperation after a frustrating two-hour loading – or should I say 'non-loading' – session happened after a 25-mile endurance ride.

Annabel's horse is a nice, sensitive little Arab mare who is actually very easy to work with. I kind of knew even before I got to the yard what I was going to find. I said to Sarah, 'What I'm going to do here is just watch Annabel with the horse. I bet she's let things go on the ground, got a bit sloppy, left a few too many decisions to the horse, and now the horse has taken the decision not to load.' Sure enough, when Annabel got the horse out of the stable and I asked her to walk around the yard, do a few turns and a few halts, I could see straight away that I was right.

I pointed out one or two things to Annabel, such as that she was walking along like she wasn't going anywhere and the horse was 'away with the fairies' whenever she felt like it, and straightaway Annabel looked at me and said, 'I've let it all go, haven't I? I can see what I've done.' A few minutes later, after Annabel had got the horse back with her, we went up to the trailer and the horse was in in less than a minute. We loaded a few more times and then Annabel rode the horse to a farm up the road and we drove up there with the trailer. The horse loaded like a dream and we all drove home.

Such a small thing made such a huge difference. It gets more like that all the time for me, and that's the way I like it. Just one more point to tack on to this little story. Going into that yard and working with Annabel but touching her horse for maybe no more than ten seconds was a really good way of doing that job. Annabel learnt a hundred times more by doing the job herself than she would have learnt by watching me doing it.

## Taking responsibility – continued

So let's look more closely at that word 'responsibility'. It's a big word with a big meaning, and so powerful too. We often give our horses far too much responsibility, which they truly do not need or want, but it is only if we proactively take up that responsibility that the horse can relinquish it. Your horse must know that you are there, taking care of all those decisions about attention, movement, direction and speed. With every horse I meet, our relationship is established by me taking the responsibility away from the horse and allowing him to feel free, and secure in the freedom I offer him.

Of course, you may not choose to do that. You may think I am wrong in what I am saying and doing. I once worked with a gentleman who really struggled with the idea that I needed the constant attention of the horse. He owned an old horse that he was only too happy to ride up the road without a care in the world, and he owned a youngster, Alf, which he had asked me to start for him. Because of this man's strong views on the subject, when I was working with Alf, I was so aware of what I was doing every time I asked for his attention that I started to feel really awkward.

To his credit, the gentleman realized I was in some conflict and we agreed it might be better if he stayed away until I'd done the job. This is not my usual way – I like the client to see and be part of what is happening, but in this case it just didn't work. So I had three days with the horse to myself and in that time I needed to get to work. Even walking Alf down the road was a nightmare because his attention was everywhere except on me. In the grass, in the hedge, lagging behind, going up ahead, bumping into me – it was awful. But that was what the owner was happy with – a completely free horse that he loved and that he thought loved him.

For those three days I walked about 20 miles with that horse, asking for his attention whenever he wandered off. I provided a nice soft place for him just behind me and to the side. Everywhere else that he went was just a tiny bit of a hassle, in that to whatever degree he chose he was walking into a tightening lead rope. On the second day, as we were on our way home I suddenly realized that things had gone very quiet. Yes, Alf had found the soft spot and, blow me, he had relaxed right into it. Once he found that special place and how nice it was, there was no looking back for Alf. We could go anywhere and do anything – he had found his home.

Alf's owner was back on the fourth day and we set off up the road for a walk. 'Wow, this is nice,' he exclaimed. 'We've never been able to walk like this before.' I couldn't resist putting in my ten pence worth and explaining how important it was for the horse to be with the handler, but I knew my words were falling on deaf ears. In the end we just had to agree to go our separate ways, because I couldn't cope with the idea of putting a rider on a horse that wasn't concentrating on what was going on.

Everyone has to choose how they want to work with their horses, and some people aren't interested in what I'm on about, but they get by to their liking with their way of doing things. Fair enough, all of us can only do what we do at the time, and all I can tell anyone about is what I am understanding at the time too. Understanding horses is not a static thing, which might just be the reason why I have got so involved in it. It's not that I think there is anything new to discover (although there might be) – I actually feel that I am walking down a well-worn path – but that as my understanding grows, and my ability to communicate with horses grows, the work I do improves. It's a good feeling.

# Winning and losing – and more about responsibility

I once had the loan of an old Welsh cob called Dylan. He was a nice old horse and I used to ride him out alongside my wife riding her horse Sam. One day we got to the bottom of the long gallop and Sarah said 'Shall we let them go?' Off we went, and we had a good race. Dylan came up alongside Sam a couple of times and each time Sam pulled ahead. We did nothing to urge either horse on so it was all their own doing. Did they want to win?

So many things that we do with our horses involve trying to win. How does that sit with taking care of the relationship between you and your horse, and is it possible to compete and still put your horse before the result?

• • •

Anna, who worked with us one year, rode Sam for a few months, and to her credit by the end of the summer he was as good as he's ever been. When the schedule for Widecombe Fair came out I suggested we put Sam in one of the classes and see how he went. The day of the fair arrived and off we went. There were ten horses in Sam's ridden cob class. Anna gave Sam an excellent ride – she is a determined girl with a healthy bit of attitude. She could see the way things were going when the judge put them down the line, so when she did her show she parked Sam up right under the judge's nose and showed that man what he could do. She threw in some nice backing up and impressive turns on the forehand and haunches, all on a light rein and nice and soft. I'm obviously biased here and cannot possibly look at this objectively, but that is not the point. The fact is that the criteria the judge had in his mind were obviously a lot different to those I had in mine. Sam was put down at the end of

*'Anna gave Sam an excellent ride. She could see the way things were going when the judge put them down the line, so when she did her show she parked Sam up right under the judge's nose and showed that man what he could do, all on a light rein and nice and soft.'*

the line and a whole bunch of horses that were being hauled in at the front with loads of ironwork and going round the ring as stiff as boards were up above him. By now steam was coming out of my wife's ears and even I was beginning to fume a little – this was so obviously wrong. 'Was it because his numnah didn't match his saddle?' I asked a good friend of mine as a joke. 'Well, numnahs are very important,' she replied in all seriousness. That was enough for me. I was out of there!

That day we went through all the emotions of competition and came away feeling pretty done over. Sam was fine about what happened though; it all went very well as far as he was concerned.

• • •

For over 30 years I have been playing an ancient Chinese board game called Go. As soon as I felt the Go stones in my hand I knew I liked the game, but what drew me towards it more than anything was that it is a game that has no luck in it whatsoever. There is no throw of the dice or cutting of the pack, your move is your responsibility and yours alone. This is very different to life, where so much happens that is beyond our control, where we can actually play very well but still lose, or where we can actually play very badly and yet by some fluke, still win.

I am not one of the best Go players in the world. I am graded at 2 kyu, which is a couple of grades below shodan, a level generally regarded as a good amateur player. In Go, the way you establish your grade is through playing in tournaments. This can be a very interesting experience on many levels. For me, trying to approach a tournament game in a detached and calm way is a huge challenge. Under the pressure of the game, the weaknesses in my character can sometimes let me down. I am technically as good as I am and in each moment I am unlikely to find a move beyond the level at which I play, but what I often do is put myself under undue stress and misread the actual situation on the board. This is something I feel I should be able to control.

Over the years I have convinced myself that I am weak in the opening of the game. Take the situation below. For this example you don't need to know the rules. I will just explain that the game is about territory – whoever controls most of the board at the end is the winner. So I am white and it is my turn. I look at the board and I'm thinking, 'Oh my goodness, I'm behind already, I really must do something urgently to get back into this game.' But look at the board again, this time calmly and objectively. Even without understanding the game, you can see that the areas of the board

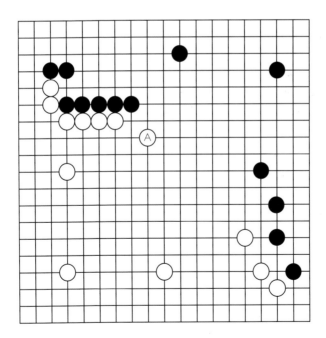

*White's next move might be at 'A' showing a clear territorial advantage*

covered with white stones are virtually equal to those covered by black stones, so why I am getting a false picture?

If I can remain calm and objective, I have so much more chance of seeing the reality of the situation and in this way I might avoid making the irrational moves that have so often led me into trouble. Over the years, my many mistimed and poorly planned invasions have cost me dear and, worse still, have opened the door to another even more disastrous weakness of mine – the panic mode. This is the state I get into when I realize I've blown it so I might as well just thrash about and hope for the best. This is no way to play Go and rarely leads to anything other than frustration and dissatisfaction.

It all sounds very familiar, and similar to the emotions we can experience with horses, doesn't it? All my feelings are magnified by the game, my desire to win and improve my grade, and suddenly I'm pitching myself into a life with some very extreme values, where victory and success are the goals at any cost. I don't want to taste defeat – that is for my opponent. Sometimes it's not so easy to lose, and out come all the excuses. As long as I fetch up with all the excuses I'll never take the responsibility, and until I take the responsibility I can never really do the job, and more importantly I can never really learn.

## Maybe you're not the responsible type

Often when I get involved in working with people I start to wonder if it could really be true that anyone can learn how to gain the trust of their horse. Let's face it, not everyone is a natural leader, or a confident person. Some of us, just by birth, feel as if we lack the qualities that it takes to convince a horse we are truly up to the job of looking after him. I can think of a few people I know who really love and understand horses, but for some reason seem totally unable to put into practice what it takes to set things up nicely with their horse.

There is some kind of block between understanding it and doing it. The scenario often goes something like this. The horse walks into their personal space and I say something along the lines of, 'Are you happy with your horse walking all over you like that?' They say 'No', so I explain that they need to find some way of showing the horse that this barginess is not acceptable. I usually suggest they stand by their horse, and when he crosses the imaginary line they should use some body language to tell him that there is a line there that they would prefer him not to cross.

So the horse gets to the line and the owner sort of shrugs and maybe makes a bit of noise, but the horse doesn't even notice and keeps on coming. The owner then looks at me as if what I'm suggesting doesn't work, or that perhaps they have a horse that is somehow different to other horses I have worked with. This is also the point where all the stuff about the horse's character comes in too: he's this kind of horse or that kind of horse; he's an alpha or a beta. No, I'm sorry guys, I just think it's all excuses because you don't want to take the responsibility for the behaviour of your horse. Do you want to be in charge of this set-up or not? You have to decide.

I then explain that they have to do whatever it takes to get the result they want. At this point they get all embarrassed and awkward about the whole thing, because they think that they just can't do it and they don't want to look stupid. Now, if any of this sounds familiar to you, you need to take some big decisions about your life and horses. This is something I had to come to terms with really early on myself. I so clearly remember being with my horse and wanting something to happen, such as wanting him to stand still for a few minutes while the farrier put some shoes on, and the only tool in my box was a prayer. Is that how it is for you? Because that's how it looks to me with some people sometimes.

> ● Don't worry about what you look like, and don't worry about making a fool of yourself. Go for it! Your horse has got to know that you are there, and he doesn't understand about any image and ego problems that might be causing you to look a bit like a limp lettuce leaf. I promise you, once you cross that barrier and feel the power that is within you, you will see another dimension to yourself. You will find the energy that horses use to communicate with each other. It is there inside you too. Without that power and commitment, your communication will be severely limited and I don't think it will ever really work.

If you don't want to be in charge in the way I am describing then that is fine. There are many ethical and practical arguments for working with horses in many different ways, and it is very important that you are comfortable with whatever way you choose to set things up between you and your horse. It is your privilege, as the human, to choose. Right now, probably more than at any other time, we have easy access to researching all sorts of ways of being with horses. The whole spectrum is there, from the big stick right through to people who believe they can actually talk to their horses in human language. Endless debates take place and countless words are written about the rights and wrongs of all the different ways. But I don't see it as 'rights and wrongs', I see it as choices that this world presents me with. I make my choice – and by the way, my choices don't have to be forever, but the important thing is that I am comfortable with them in each moment.

I know that it is easy to say these things and often not so easy to do them, but if you are serious about your horse work then taking steps towards freeing yourself from your ego is going to be a real step in the right direction. Think about all the trainers you enjoy watching – one of the best things is the way that they are not under pressure from their own minds. They are there working with the horse, almost unaware of what the people around them are thinking. If your mind is concentrating on your image or how your performance is going or how it looks, then all that energy is being misdirected away from the horse. That cannot be good. As time goes by and your confidence grows it will become easier for you to focus on the real job – after all it is what you and your horse both want.

# ●Useful qualities

*I want to dedicate this book to all the people reading it who, like me, didn't know how to get on with horses. I hope that some of what I have written will help improve the relationship between you and the horses that you meet in your life. I have watched, and am still watching, how people are with horses and how horses are with people, and there is no doubt in my mind that it is no fluke that I am getting on better with horses now than I used to.*

Horses are simple animals with simple needs, and you do not need to be a rocket scientist to get on with most of them. Of course, if you are a rocket scientist then that should not be a problem either, but sadly sometimes it can be. Sometimes we human beings, blessed with these hugely complicated brains, just don't actually want things to be simple, and sometimes all that cleverness can just make things a tad more confusing than perhaps they should be. The qualities that horses are looking for in humans are not linked to intellect or education. They are simple qualities like clarity, patience, consistency, fairness and generosity. These are all things that we can work on within ourselves, and maybe we will need to if we want to go down this road.

● **Clarity** comes from understanding. Understand the horse. Take on board the principle that the horse's number one instinct in life is survival, and all of his actions are centred around this instinct. Abandon the idea that horses think like humans. Abandon all these crazy notions about horses being naughty and 'taking the mickey'. These are concepts that are so far from the truth it's almost laughable, and they are also extremely unhelpful. If you find yourself thinking in this way, stop for a moment, think seriously about the true nature of the horse and try to work out what is really going on. Coming from this new viewpoint, slowly work towards your goal. You may have to work things out consciously to start with, but soon your understanding of the horse will become second nature. You will start to see the true motivation behind your horse's actions, and from there your progress will be immense.

● **Patience** is a useful quality to develop, and your horse will thank you for it. Take on board that some things do not happen with the flick of a switch. For sure, every now and again someone will come by with a new tip that might get you a bit of a result, but the real stuff takes time. For you, and your horse, don't be in a hurry. Sometimes the goal becomes so important and so urgent that the true destination becomes obscured. In reality, your true destination is here, now. It's not some place down the road, just out of sight, that you never seem to reach. Get into that moment with your horse – he's there waiting for you. And then, in time, the long-term goals you have set for yourself and your horse will emerge, not just in your imagination but in reality.

● **Consistency** Many people talk about being consistent, but what they often forget to say is that they mean being consistently good, not consistently bad. However, for the sake of your horse, consistently bad is probably preferable to being consistently erratic – that sometimes messes horses up big time. Horses have good memories. If they get one response to one thing one day and a different response to the same thing the next day, the next time they will face that same situation with anxiety and apprehension. For me, this is all about pressure and release, and providing a soft place for the horse to be when he's getting things right. Those are the parts of his language that I use. But that is just for me: ultimately, whatever training methods or concepts you work with, consistency is surely a must. The language of the horse is not difficult for us to work with; I'm pretty sure we don't need to learn some complicated great dictionary of horse speak. If you just learn the bit that you need, as a human being, to work with your horse, and practise keeping your asks and your responses consistent, then you will get there.

● **Fairness** Take on board that it is unfair to ask your horse to do something that he doesn't understand, or that he is frightened of doing. Know in your heart that if you do ask your horse to do either of these things, you have made all the efforts you possibly can beforehand to help eliminate the misunderstanding or fear that your horse is experiencing. How will you know? Your horse will be calm, and will be conscious of what he is doing. Flight and panic will not be on his agenda.

● **Generosity** Make sure that there is always something in it for your horse. It has to be worth his while. Have your horse do things for you because he wants to out of trust and respect. That will come about by you giving him what is, to him, a good, logical reason to choose the option you are asking for. Keep your horse sweet this way too. Make life make sense for your horse. Don't keep batting away at the same meaningless-to-the-horse exercises that get your horse nowhere. Don't run the risk of turning him sour. Give him what he wants from you and he will give back to you what you want from him.

'For me, this is all about pressure and release, and providing a soft place for the
horse to be when he's getting things right. Those are the parts of his language that
I use. If you just learn the bit that you need to work with your horse, and practise
keeping your asks and your responses consistent, then you will get there.'

# Is that too many rules?

● Throughout this book I have tried not to put in too many do's and don't's. Don't come to me and say that I said you should have done this or that, so you did it, and everything went wrong. You must take all the responsibility for everything you do – all of it, absolutely 100 percent. Every decision you take is yours. If someone standing beside you tells you to do something, you choose whether to do it or not. It's your choice. I'm not going to give you one rule (well, maybe one), or one method, or one technique that I say you should use, because it is your choice.

Who knows what is around the corner? Make a rule, break a rule – that's the age-old maxim of life, isn't it? We've all seen the high moralists come unstuck by their own desires. I've been there, that's for sure.

So try not to get caught up in any rules and concepts, because as sure as horses are horses, the situation will come along where you will have to break your rule. If you vow never, ever to use fear with a horse, then how are you going to turn away a charging stallion, or avoid being crushed or kicked by an unruly youngster? Keep an open mind, but aim for the best.

*And now here is the only rule you should never break:*

## STAY SAFE

Working with horses is not like playing on a computer – I've done that and the potential for getting hurt is not high. If you find yourself in dangerous situations that you really feel you have to deal with, then take care to minimize the risks. A lot of it is obvious, like wearing a safety hat, working in a smaller or safer area, or having a competent friend to help you. These are easy things to organize. Beyond that, I look at danger almost as a consequence of approaching the job in the wrong way – maybe I am asking for too much too soon; maybe I can ask for less or explain things better to the horse. If I work within the boundaries of what the horse can cope with, then I can help to minimize the chances of experiencing that 'western moment', as it is sometimes known.

# •Solving problems

*When I started writing this book, I was determined not to make lists. I just don't like them, because for me working with horses is not about having a list. As things have worked out, I've already made one list and here is another. This list covers some of the common problems that people present themselves with when they are working with their horses. If you spot any of the following in yourself, then think about it for a while, be conscious of it and try not to let it interfere with your work. Search for the solution within yourself – it's in there, so get into the habit of looking for it.*

## Learned helplessness

**⑦Problem** You are at a show and your horse is behaving very badly. You have one of your friends there with you who you know is good enough with horses to help you. Instead of looking for a solution yourself, your main aim is to pass the problem on to your friend as quickly as possible.

**✔ Solution** Try to spot yourself doing this, and then work out how you would get yourself out of the situation you are in with your horse if your friend wasn't there.

## Inexperience

**⑦Problem** You are riding a young horse and he is losing his motivation and appears to be becoming bored. This doesn't seem to happen when your much more experienced friend gets on the same horse.

✅ **Solution** Be proactive, use your imagination and give the horse a 'job' to do – don't just leave him 'hanging there'. Sometimes it's as simple as that, and you thought it was some magic ingredient you didn't have! It's not, it's just experience.

## Too many concepts

❓ **Problem** You are unsuccessfully trying to get your horse to back up and it is turning into an ugly sight. You are combining all that you ever learnt, so what's going wrong?

✅ **Solution** Some of the stuff you have learnt is not correct. Keep it simple and don't go where you don't understand. Does it make sense to you? Is it easy? A 'yes' to both of these questions is usually a good indication that you are on the right track.

## Getting stuck

❓ **Problem** You have an unhandled youngster and you can't get beyond stroking him on his hindquarters.

✅ **Solution** The place that you are stuck is in your mind. Use your imagination and find a way through. For example, you could try using a stick with a soft rag wrapped around the end of it, so that you can advance the contact up his back without moving your body further into his personal space. Always look for the next small step.

## Horses don't like you

❓ **Problem** Your horse prefers it when you are not around. He is dismissive of you and only reacts if you shout or get heavy. You have a deep-seated belief that he is trying to do you down.

✅ **Solution** It's not true. Your belief is causing you to be defensive, aggressive and over-demanding. Horses are mirrors – you get out what you put in. Try to approach your horse with a slightly more sympathetic attitude and see if you can swing things around the opposite way.

### Getting heavy

**❓ Problem** You take on board all the good stuff about softness and feel, but as time goes you gradually slip back into your old ways.

**✅ Solution** Stay in touch – watch other people work, watch videos, read books. The human condition is to drift – if you hear yourself saying things like, 'It's all very well, but sometimes...' you probably need to get back on track.

### Perfectionism

**❓ Problem** You become dispirited because you can't get it right. You take the imperfection personally.

**✅ Solution** I live with a perfectionist and I love her, but sometimes it drives me up the wall. How many times have I heard her say, 'No, that's not right'? So what if it takes a few days to get to where you want to be? What's the hurry? Sometimes it works well just to settle for the smallest thing in the right direction. It'll come.

### Slackness

**❓ Problem** You are sloppy in your work because you settle for less than perfection.

**✅ Solution** Yep, that's me. Sometimes horses need to be pushed on towards perfection. It sharpens up their act and gets them right on track. When I work with Sarah, it's a bit like 'good cop, bad cop' – I soften them up, then she goes in and gets all the glory.

### Too much theory

**❓ Problem** Paralysis by analysis – I just hate it.

**✅ Solution** Leave me alone to be with my horse.

### Beating yourself up

**❓ Problem** You are gently trying to encourage your horse not to be so frightened of having his halter put on. Things are going really well, and then you approach him just a bit more quickly than he can cope with. He runs off with the halter half on, and off you go: 'Oh no, I don't believe I did that, I'm so rubbish...'

✔ **Solution** When things go wrong, don't even begin to go to this godforsaken area of your mind. These things just happen: for sure you should try to learn from them, you'd be stupid not to. But one thing is certain: you won't learn anything helpful from wallowing in your own self-pity. Crack on and get back to the job in hand.

## Fear of failure

❓ **Problem** 'I know I won't be able to do it, so I'm not even going to try.' You are asked whether you would like to demonstrate your horse skills at the local pony club. You decline, because there is a real possibility that things may go wrong and you will look very silly.

✔ **Solution** There's some wisdom in this – set yourself up for a winner and all that – it makes sense to me. But there is a difference between fear of failure because your ego is very fragile, and failing at something because that is something that happens occasionally. If you think you have something to offer then just go for it, otherwise you'll never get out of the house. When that ego dies, freedom follows.

## Wishy-washyness

❓ **Problem** 'If I'm firm, my horse won't like me.' Or perhaps it's more like 'I'm too shy or embarrassed in case it doesn't work', or 'I can't do that because I might look a bit stupid'. (But not as stupid as you look at the moment, with a horse that hasn't got a clue because you haven't either.)

✔ **Solution** Horses need clear, black-and-white situations with no grey areas. Give this to your horse – no excuses. If you are truly wishy-washy and are utterly convinced that this is the real, unchangeable you, then maybe you should seriously consider another hobby. It's not fair to your horse. Really, it's not so difficult, and with a bit of effort and the appropriate horse, then you can have a horse. But with no effort at all, then you can't, and that's the law!

## Can't put theory into practice

**? Problem** 'I read in a book how to do it but it just isn't working.'

**✔ Solution** Books are great, but they are just books. It's a bit like eating a recipe to try to stave off your hunger. It doesn't work: you have to have real food. Get out there and watch real people working with real horses, and start to do it yourself. Get yourself a good teacher whom you understand and respect, and who understands and respects you. How do you know that what you are being taught is good? Because it works. There should be no mystery about working with horses.

## How do you judge when you've done enough?

**? Problem** You are getting on really well with handling your previously untouched yearling. You have managed to rub him all up his neck and he will now let you stand at his side. Should you carry on while things are going well, or should you stop and carry on tomorrow?

**✔ Solution** I don't know. You have to decide by how you feel. Sometimes it's definitely a good idea to keep going when you are on a roll and at other times it pays to go more slowly. If you make the wrong decision, generally it won't matter too much – maybe you'll make the right one next time. How do you know it's the wrong decision, anyway? You don't know what would have happened if you had gone with the opposite decision.

## My horse gets cross when I work with him

**? Problem** Your horse has a problem with you picking up his back feet. He's fine for a while but then he becomes very irritable and is obviously getting annoyed with you. Should you stop or carry on?

**✔ Solution** When your horse gets cross with you it's a symptom of a not-so-good relationship between the two of you. I would look to be working this out over time rather than necessarily facing it head on (literally!) when it happens. He is asking you the question 'Who is in charge here? Who is taking the decisions?' He is not convinced that it should be you. Carry on working on setting up the relationship in areas where it is safe, like leading or loose work, rather than dealing with the issue around his back feet. Or, if you have enough experience, you could use working on the problem to help set up the relationship...

## I'm not in the right place

**? Problem** 'When I watch you work and things go wrong, you always seem to be in the right place to do something about it. At the show yesterday, when my horse got very over-excited, I felt that I was always one move behind where I needed to be.'

**✔ Solution** When I first started hanging around with horses, I marvelled at how relaxed people were with them. Then I realized that after a while I could almost feel where they were going to move next; I could somehow just keep myself in the right place. It comes down to experience, and of course I'm not always in the right place either. Sometimes you have to move there and fast, and sometimes you get it wrong. It's a bit like watching a good rider sitting on a difficult horse – they don't think about it, they just do it. It's just experience. But one thing that does help hugely is to establish your personal space – a lot of the feeling of not being in the right place is simply because you are being crowded out by your horse.

### Lack of confidence

**❓ Problem** 'I don't have much confidence, should I give up now?'

**✅ Solution** Go in at a level with which you can cope. Getting the right horse can be a big help. If you are worried about big horses, get a small one. If you are worried about fast horses, get a slow one. If you are worried about picking up feet, get a horse that has no problem picking up his feet. There is a horse out there for everyone, or is that just a dream? I honestly don't think it is, but go steady, be wise, and hopefully get lucky.

# Remember – we are all human

Sometimes when people watch me working they say things along the lines of how good it is to watch someone who understands horses, but if they ever start to infer that it is some kind of special gift, I always stop them right there. I have in me all the same stuff that every horse person has in them, and all the same stuff that every other person in this world – whoever they are – has in them too. Once or twice I have rubbed shoulders with the rich and famous, and also with the incredibly poor or disadvantaged people in this world, and I have always been acutely aware of the similarities in our predicament. Without exception, we all face life and death, success and failure, being liked and disliked, and the search for a meaning to this life. None of these things is affected by wealth, fame or worldly skills of any kind. The things that really matter in life are no different for any of us. We're all just somewhere different on the spectrum of the human experience – we get used to where we are and work from there.

With horse work, the levels of confidence, the search for a way of doing things, the success or the lack of it – wherever you are on the spectrum of horsemanship, it's all in there. And don't you just feel that downside so strongly when you come away from a situation knowing that you haven't really got things going in the right direction? I bet you could take the world's best horse trainers, and in their most honest moments they would have to admit that they have felt it too. It's a human feeling, and I have a hunch that to be good with horses you need to realize that you are human and know that these feelings are just part of living in this world.

So, next time you hear someone say any of the following, stop and think. I do.

'Oh, he's marvellous with horses.'
'Oh, he just seems to have a way with horses.'
'Oh, horses just seem to relax in his presence.'
'Oh, when he talks, horses just seem to melt.'
'Oh, horses seem to know he's OK.'
'Oh, horses just seem to understand what he wants.'

Just remember, it could be *you* they're talking about, really it could be, and actually it should be, for the sake of your horse.

⬤ It's not some mysterious gift that makes it happen that way between a human and a horse. Of course, it might be a mystery to the person who sees it as a gift, but it won't be a mystery to me. I have looked and looked at people and horses and what I have learnt about how to be with horses is all down to my and other people's practical observations of what is actually happening between the human and the horse. It's nothing new, that's for sure, and with a bit of serious effort we can all be that same way. That would be nice for the horses, wouldn't it?

# • Be with your horse

*So there is a way of being with horses that they really understand. If we can be that way then the horse will feel it and relax. I know this is true because I experience it over and over again. When I meet a horse, any horse, I go in there with one aim: to find that experience between me and the horse, where we can both get along and get some work done.*

If you have never felt this thing, then I recommend that you have a go at feeling it. Not for one moment am I saying that without it being with horses is no fun, because patently that isn't true. But truly being with your horse lifts the whole experience into another dimension. Suddenly true communication is there, suddenly there are no barriers, suddenly two beings are working as one: it is that 'magic' experience that changes everything.

I hope that while reading this book you have either recognized this experience in your own life, or perhaps recognized it happening for others and realized that you would like to feel it too. I hope I have inspired you to make it a priority in the time that you spend with horses. If you are feeling in any way that you are almost catching a glimpse of something but can't quite get it, then whatever you do, don't think that it can't happen for you. It most definitely can.

Find a good teacher – he or she will be able to help you find that feeling. When you feel it, don't just dismiss it – see it as the beginning and nurture it. Make it your priority and go back for more. One day that desire will become your default in your work with horses. It's not some mystical experience that's on ration. It is in fact available

in an infinite supply. Some people are naturally there but for most of us it does take effort and dedication. It is so worth making that effort. Once I couldn't see it at all, then I could see it in other people, then I felt it myself. From there I wanted to feel it more, and now I sometimes feel like a small bee that has found an absolutely huge pile of honey beyond my wildest dreams.

Of course it's only horses but there's just something about horses isn't there?

# Get it into your mind how it is for the horse

I ended up at the farm with Ed, the hay contractor, and his two young daughters. One of the girls was just horse mad. She wanted to see every horse I had and needed to know all their names, how old they were and what they were doing.

On the way back to the car, she started to tell me about one of the horses at the riding school where she was learning her stuff. 'he gets really cross, he bites all the time and kicks out with his feet. He's a really horrible horse.'

Without thinking, I just said, 'I'm sure he's got his reasons.'

Ed looked round, thought about it for a second and said, 'I guess he must have.'

I hope you've enjoyed reading this book; I've enjoyed writing it.